YOUR GUIDE TO INVESTING IN THE URBAN REAL ESTATE MARKET

Copyright © 2023

All rights reserved. No portion of this book may be reproduced, distributed, or transmitted in any form by photocopying, recording electronically or mechanically, or by any information storage, without the prior written permission of the publisher.

The information provided herein is stated to be truthful and consistent, in that any liability, in terms of inattention or otherwise, by any usage or abuse of any policies, processes, or directions contained within is the solitary and utter responsibility of the recipient reader. Under no circumstances will any legal responsibility or blame be held against the publisher for any reparation, damages, or monetary loss due to the information herein, either directly or indirectly.

Respective author owns all copyrights not held by the publisher. The information herein is offered for informational purposes solely, and is universal as so. The presentation of the information is without contract or any type of guarantee assurance.

For permission requests, write to the author or the Publisher addressed, Attention: WMYL Publishing

WMYL Publishing

PO Box 21512

South Euclid, Ohio 44121

Printed in the United States of America

First printing edition 2023

ISBN: 979-8-218-95196-2

Dedication

To Laura A. Thompson:

Mom, you always said I should write a book. And you always made us feel loved. This is for you.

Acknowledgements

Gary L. Martin:

I'm a little upset that you weren't involved in this whole process but it's all good....

(He'll get the reference)

Table of Contents

INTRODUCTION 1

CHAPTER ONE: DEFINING THE URBAN MARKET 5

CHAPTER TWO: WEALTH AND FREEDOM MINDSET 16

CHAPTER THREE: DUE DILIGENCE.. 23

CHAPTER FOUR: FINANCING 43

CHAPTER FIVE: TENANTS 57

CHAPTER SIX: BUILDING A TEAM 81

CHAPTER SEVEN: CONCLUSION 101

INTRODUCTION

It was February 28th at two in the morning. It was wintertime, one of the coldest days ever in Cleveland; negative 30 degrees to be exact. One of my tenants was blowing up my phone the evening before, telling me they could not get the heat on, and they also had a sewer backup. It turned out to be a long night for everyone. I called one of my contractors, and we headed over there around 10pm and spent nearly five hours trying to rectify the problems—only for me to have to be up early the next morning to go to work. I remember being so frustrated with these tenants because they had been flushing chicken grease down the toilet, which now had led to damage in the basement sewer drain. I could not believe my eyes when the contractor put his hand down the drain to locate where the blockage was. I stood stunned and grossed out. He was struggling and looked over to me and motioned for help. I went from a dazed look to a "fuck it, let's get the job done" attitude. I quickly moved near him, and there I was with my arm elbow deep in the drain too. It is still very vivid in my mind. I literally had my whole arm down in shit. Yes, you heard right. Shit. Human made, foul smelling, straight out this tenant's large intestines shit. I will never forget how grimy I felt. I don't know how that episode led to me deciding that I would be in real estate for the long haul, but I looked at my arm that day and knew there was no turning back.

I got into real estate over fifteen years ago when I bought my first property. When I married my wife a few years later, we took a huge leap of faith and both quit our jobs to continue growing our portfolio. She was nine months pregnant with our first child at the time. We emptied our 401(k)s to buy more properties. We thought things would be smooth, but in the first month, we had an underground waterline burst at one of our rentals. Fixing it cost us ten thousand dollars! Imagine the fear and anxiety we were feeling at the time; we were under so much pressure with so much riding on us to make it as full-time investors and now new parents.

I'll never forget lying next to her one night when she suddenly burst into tears. We were both scared because we had no idea what the future held. Without having to ask her what was wrong, I simply put my arm around her knowing that we were both overwhelmed with the same fear.

If you have recently invested in real estate and are scared, I know how you feel. You are not alone; it is probably how every investor feels when entering the real estate market at some level. You will throw in your hard-earned money—for some it will be all you have—only to wonder if this dream you have will work out. You will be unsure, and that's okay. What matters is you are taking a step toward your goals, and the fact you are reading this book indicates you are willing to put in the work needed. You can do this.

For the last eight years, I've owned and operated a full service real estate brokerage and property management company called Monument Real Estate Services. Monument manages nearly 400 residential homes primarily in the Cleveland, Ohio, area as well as several in Columbus, OH, and Charlotte, NC. Investors from all over the world trust us to help them buy and sell investment properties and to manage them on their behalf. While managing residential assets for hundreds of investor clients over the years, I have seen them experience plenty of losses, frustrations, mistakes, miscalculations, and getting taken advantage of. I've also witnessed their wins, excitement, spot on execution, and portfolio growth. A few years ago, I was talking with one of my peers in the industry, and we swapped a few stories about our day to day with the investors we work with. We noticed a similar thread between them. Most of them are making the same mistakes, aren't doing their due diligence, and don't understand the urban markets they are investing in. I realized that investors need a certain level of education and guidance before they put their money and hopes into real estate. I decided to write this book to counsel and help real estate investors circumvent the challenges that will lie ahead. And, to be honest, I need to get all of this information out of my head before I go crazy. I believe I have a lot of value to share and that it's my duty to deliver it to those who need it.

Over the next several chapters, I will be your guide. I will educate you on how to fulfill your dream of investing in real estate. Together, we will go over key strategies for investing successfully. You will learn which properties to purchase, where, and how to buy them. You will also learn how to build the right relationships with your tenants, contractors, and property managers to ensure success. More importantly, you will understand why investing in the urban market differs from investing in other types of markets. This book will be your complete guide to investing in the urban real estate market.

CHAPTER ONE

Defining the Urban Market

I have defined the urban real estate market as being located in a **low economic** community, with older homes that often have **deferred maintenance**, and having high levels of **government compliance**. It is often synonymous with the inner-city, or colloquialisms such as the hood, the ghetto, and war zone. When people talk about "war zones" in particular, I truly feel it's an exaggeration that is overused by people who have never been to these areas. These cities are not Iraq or Afghanistan with bombs going off every day. Although you'll often find more crime, you'll typically find it's regulated to specific streets or sections of a community.

Residents of neighborhoods in the urban market tend to be mostly minorities and less educated than other cities on the national average. Many of these cities are located in the Midwest and Southern regions of the United States. Investors often love to purchase in these neighborhoods because the prices of homes are typically lower than in other areas, and the rate of return is usually better than other traditional avenues of investing.

The urban market is what most investors might describe as C&D markets. You'll find in real estate, an informal letter grade scale has been adopted by many that generally helps an investor more easily define a city or neighborhood based on specific characteristics and demographics. Typically, C&D markets have lower economic conditions such as high unemployment, more crime, and people with less education. In contrast, A&B markets are suburban, more affluent, have lower crime rates, lower unemployment, more educated people, and overall would be deemed as more desirable. Throughout this book, I'll refer to C & D markets and the urban real estate market interchangeably. Although this grading scale is useful in helping to quickly categorize neighborhoods, this type of rating system has also been a double-edged sword when it comes to discriminatory practices such as steering and red lining.

As I mentioned before, three things define the urban market, showing that it differs significantly from A&B markets. They are:

1. The low economic nature of the market.
2. The deferred maintenance of homes.
3. The high level of compliance with government policies required in the municipalities.

1. The Low Economic Nature of the Market

The low economic nature of an area is one of the most significant factors when defining an urban real estate market. Residents of neighborhoods in urban areas, statistically, have less formal levels of education than on the national average, and lower levels of education typically lead to lower paying jobs and higher poverty. Residents also, on average, have larger families and usually have extended family members living with them. Also, low economic conditions are often coupled with crime. This isn't to make a blanket statement that crime is rampant everywhere in the urban market, but when you break down the numbers per capita, you'll find higher crime as compared to A&B real estate markets.

So, what does this mean to you as an investor in the urban market? You must understand how these conditions affect the people who live there and the unique challenges you'll face as a landlord. Higher poverty generally means you'll have more transient tenants. This means shorter occupancy rates are more common. You'll, on average, have higher delinquencies and nonpayment of rent because more tenants are living paycheck to paycheck. You may find you have higher turnover costs when preparing the property for a new tenant because the property usually has more wear and tear. You'll find quality, reliable contractors are harder to come by, and fewer traditional lenders are willing to lend on properties that are only worth $50,000. All of this will affect everything from the condition of your property to the contractors and lenders that you work with. I'll go more in depth about all of this in later chapters, but know for now that the low economic conditions have a vast effect on your investment strategy. You must have a complete understanding of the major role it plays in how you, as an investor, maneuver the urban market.

In this book, I will mostly talk about Cleveland, OH, one of the top urban real estate markets in the US. However, for general insight into the urban real estate market, this basic knowledge will apply to other similar areas such as Memphis, Indianapolis, Birmingham, St. Louis, and Detroit. In the table below, you will find the rates of specific characteristics of the urban market in these areas as compared to the national average.

Statistics on Cities in the Urban Real Estate Market in Comparison with the National Average

National Average	Cleveland	Detroit	Memphis	Indianapolis	Birmingham
Home Price	63% lower	78% lower	49% lower	35% lower	53% lower
Crime	144% higher	130% higher	237% higher	89% higher	251% higher
Employment/Pay	40% lower	48% lower	24% lower	16% lower	30% lower
Education	30% lower	61% lower	57% lower	32% lower	100% lower

2. The Deferred Maintenance of Homes

Deferred maintenance is the second defining factor of properties in the urban real estate market. One thing you have to understand is that homes in this market are generally older—some even 70, 80, or 90 plus years old. Naturally, with older homes comes more maintenance and updates that are required. I find that many of the investors I work with are highly sensitive about being called "slum" lords., and many do what is needed to properly maintain their investments. However, I frequently see that major repairs, such as roofs, HVAC systems, plumbing, or renovations are often deferred due to cost. Additionally, because investors want to maximize their income, they often find contractors who don't do quality work. On top of that, it can be a challenge to find quality, reliable contractors who are willing to do work in these areas, so identifying one early on will be crucial.

Many properties in urban markets have been used as rental properties for decades and decades, transferring ownership several times, and housing dozens and dozens of families over the years. Because of this, you'll naturally have more wear and tear of properties and often more neglect as tenants traditionally don't maintain a home the same way an owner occupant would.

3. The High Level of Government Compliance

A higher level of compliance with government policies goes into owning and managing properties in the urban real estate market. Compared to A&B markets, investors have to deal with everything from the housing courts and evictions, city inspectors, local councils, and more rules and regulations. Bottom line—this means more money out of your pocket.

Housing voucher programs are a very common encounter with government compliance that many investors have. The most well-known program many are familiar with is called Section 8. It's known as Section 8 because Section 8 of the Housing Act of 1937 authorized payment of rental housing assistance to private landlords on behalf of low-income households in the US.

Programs like this allow tenants to subsidize their cost of living, often leading to a win-win for both landlords and tenants. This program guarantees a portion of rent will be paid every month to landlords, and it allows tenants to live in suitable housing at a lower cost.

With many voucher programs, there are guidelines that must be followed regarding the condition, health, and safety of the property.

If you choose to utilize these programs, the process can be capital and administratively intensive when you first get started in order to meet these guidelines. However, once you've procured a tenant, it does create a more turnkey investment because of the guaranteed payments.

When we talk about government compliance, it is important to understand each local municipality and their unique requirements for rental properties and landlords. For instance, in the city of Cleveland, where we primarily manage properties, all rental properties are required to be registered with the city. There's a cost per unit to register, and it must be completed every year. This is likely to give the city a good grasp on the ratio of housing that is being rented versus owner occupied. This data could be used for various reasons. Or, some of the more cynical critics may say it's just a money grab for the city to create an income line item in their budget. Either way, it's their rule, and you have to follow it.

Another example of government compliance within the city of Cleveland is their newly enacted lead-based paint certification requirement. This initiative was introduced to increase the safety of families in rental properties throughout the city who may be living in potentially unsafe conditions as a direct result of deferred maintenance. Lead-based paint was used before the 1970s because it kept paint fresh and the colors brighter, and it was often used in homes and even on children's toys. It was later discovered that lead-based paint was highly toxic and caused developmental issues in children. In 1978, the US government banned the manufacture of this paint; however, it is still prevalent in many older homes. The city of Cleveland now requires all rental properties to be lead-safe certified and have an approved inspector remove any lead hazards in homes.

I mention these programs because it's important to understand the rules and regulations of the urban markets you are investing in so you can prepare for the associated costs and be educated on your requirements as a landlord.

WHAT THE URBAN REAL ESTATE MARKET IS NOT

Because the word "urban" can be ambiguous or have multiple meanings, I want to explain what I mean when I use this term. When I talk about urban, you must consider population, home values, and crime and unemployment rates. While the word urban can be used to describe densely populated cities, this isn't the only factor considered when we discuss the urban real estate market.

However, size matters. Smaller cities with populations less than 300,000 are not considered urban real estate markets. A market that's not deemed urban will have properties valued at the national average or above. It will also have at or above national average rents with tenants that can afford to pay. This tends to minimize the need for government assistance. The properties in these areas are typically newer with less deferred maintenance, and the quality of tenant is better because they are more financially stable. For these purposes, cities like Miami, Los Angeles, San Diego, San Jose, Washington D.C., and Boston may be urban because they are large metropolitan cities, but they are not defined as urban real estate markets. Prices are higher, meaning they are more capital intensive to purchase and rate of returns are smaller. In an urban market, your return on investment could be anywhere between 30% and 50%, whereas in non-urban markets it could be as small as 10%.

Let's look at the following cities to further help define an urban market.

Atlanta, GA—Has a large population, but low levels of government compliance and higher home values. Not an urban real estate market.

Queens, NY—Has a large population as well as high government compliance and low economic conditions, but the home values are higher than the national average which disqualifies it as an urban market.

Chicago, IL—Has deferred maintenance for many of its homes, a large population, and high levels of government compliance.

However, just like Queens, NY, and Atlanta, GA, the home values are high; therefore, this would not be considered an urban real estate market.

Canton, OH—Has high government compliance, low economic conditions, and home values are below the national average; but with a population less than 100,000, it doesn't meet the urban market criteria.

As you can see, all three criteria—low economic nature, deferred home maintenance, and high government compliance—as well as population requirements and low home values are all necessary for a city to qualify as an urban real estate market.

Investing in A&B markets are what some people might consider a safer investment. There's a lower probability that things will go wrong from a property management standpoint. However, the capital needed to invest in these markets compared to the rate of return yields a safer investment with a smaller profit.

Investment in A&B markets is highly regulated, as investors mostly deal with professionals and specialists. This makes investing here a relatively smooth journey, much more straightforward than you have in C&D markets. Investing in A&B markets is what most people consider a 'safe' investment because there is a lower probability that things will go wrong. The cash flow is stronger because people who live in these neighborhoods are often educated professionals and specialists with higher incomes. Also, properties are usually in high demand amongst a broad range of investors. This can drive the prices beyond the means of the average investor. Also, there tends to be less government oversight in these areas, so investors do not have as many rules and policies to comply with.

SUMMARY

In summary, the urban real estate market is defined by three factors:

- The low economic nature of the market.
- The deferred maintenance of homes.
- The high level of compliance with government policies.

Investing in the urban real estate market significantly differs from investing in A&B markets because of these three factors. It's a good idea to research a city's specific rules and regulations for landlords and rental properties, because these will dictate what you can and cannot do, and what you are required to do, which can mean more cost to you. When choosing a property, understand that many homes in this market will be older and may require more maintenance and repairs. Make sure you understand dynamics that a weak economy has on a city in C&D markets and how that affects your property value, your tenants, your cash flow, and unexpected variables that you may face as an investor. At the core, you are taking on more inherent risks, but the potential to yield high returns is there.

The word 'urban' when we talk about the urban real estate market does not mean necessarily downtown, big city. Population and home values play a big part in determining if a city is in an urban real estate market.

CHAPTER TWO

Wealth and Freedom Mindset

Why are we here? Why are you reading this book when you could be doing anything else? I'll tell you why. It is because likely you want to be wealthy and free. Wealth transcribes to security, and freedom is your time. When you break it down to its lowest denominator, this is what almost all of us desire.

When I talk about wealth in terms of real estate investing, I think of long term. It allows you to create and build upon your legacy even when you are no longer on this earth. Some of you look at investing in real estate as a vehicle to grow a portfolio that can fund a diverse array of other investments, and tax write-offs that will yield long-term dividends. And there isn't just one definition of wealth. Sure, you have the billionaires of the world like Jay-Z, Oprah Winfrey, or Aliko Dangote who have more money and financial wealth than most of us would know what to do with. Financial security is in the eye of the wallet holder. While some aspire to enjoy yachts in the Mediterranean, others may aspire to make sure all of their bills are paid and have extra left to put into savings each month. Both are completely incredible, because in both scenarios, each person enjoys happiness and peace of mind on their terms.

But we also know true wealth can be defined as using your money, time, and influence to help others and not just yourself.

Freedom on the other hand is a feeling. It's the here and now. You may only have a few properties, but it provides you the ability to do other things you want to do. That could be paying for a child's education or not having to work as many hours each week at your job. Time and your ability to choose how to spend it can provide a security that garners a true state of happiness. Real estate investing is great in that it can lead you to both wealth and freedom.

When I was working in corporate America, I saw and met a lot of successful people. However, sometimes the challenge for me was that most of these people had spent many, many years to get to that level of success. And also in Corporate America, I saw people struggling day to day, hating their jobs. One of the lowest feelings I've had is feeling like I could contribute more to an organization but wasn't able to because of nepotism, bureaucracy, and implicit biases. Having that feeling made me really want to make sure that I not only had multiple streams of income, but a primary one that allowed me to bet on myself and see how far my talents, intellect, and hard work could take me.

You need to believe in yourself, and I'm not talking about being cocky. It's believing in your own God-given abilities with an unwavering faith. I didn't always have this mindset, and it didn't really set in for me until I was in my 30s. That's when I started to believe I could achieve whatever career or financial goal I set. Even when the setbacks came, it was the grace of God that kept me going.

While working my corporate job, I was lucky enough to have a few friends and acquaintances that were working full time investing in real estate. I'm reminded of a guy I knew in college who I had kept in touch with throughout the years. He became a real estate agent and constantly exposed me to his growth in real estate, from brokering deals to owning properties of his own, and the differences in the strategies of buy and hold versus fix and flip. I bought my first property from him. When you see someone doing it, it becomes easier to see yourself doing it too.

Seeing other investors my age made me want to do this full time. Most don't do this full time, nor will they ever. And trust me, you don't have to. The main goal is to acquire at least one property to begin building the foundation for the wealth and freedom you didn't have before.

Before getting into real estate, I reconditioned my mind because I knew succeeding in it would require a different mindset. As I pointed out in the last chapter, the urban market is unlike any market you have likely seen, and that's why it needs a different approach. I learned and made a lot of mistakes over the last decade, and I'm battle tested. If you have been holding back from investing in real estate because of the fear of making a mistake, or the fear of losing money, or the fear of not knowing what to do or where to start, I'm here to show you that holding on to that fear will not help you achieve your goals.

I know this fear because I've seen it in the people around me. For years I've tried to get many of my family members to invest in real estate and allow me to show them the ropes. Those who agreed to take the step eventually reaped the benefits. Those who didn't held on to their fears. Imagine how frustrating it can be to have the people closest to you see your accomplishments and be so fearful that all they do is admire it when they could easily obtain the same fulfilment themselves.

A lot of this comes down to taking a risk. Many think of real estate as risky compared to a 9-to-5 career, but I don't think people always understand how risky their current situation actually is. For example, look at most of the jobs where people feel at ease. Anyone in sales will tell you, you are only as safe as your last quarter's numbers. Anyone in logistics would tell you most companies are looking for ways to be lean and efficient, which usually leads to job cuts. Anyone in retail or the hospitality industry will tell you that the volatility of the economy, or even, as we have recently experienced, a pandemic can mean you are out of work in a heartbeat. There's also technology or business mergers and acquisitions that occur all the time and pose a threat to our workforce. So, bottom line, while most people rest comfortably behind their consistent, bi-weekly paycheck, they never know how close they are to being let go. I don't say this to scare you, but rather to inspire you to make sure you have multiple avenues of income that will be longer lasting and possibly more fulfilling than your job.

Most often the best scenario is to marry your 9-to-5 with your real estate investment ambitions. You may not be in a position to leave your job, and leaving may not actually be your best option. Sure I jumped headfirst and ten toes deep into the real estate game when we left our jobs to pursue it full time, but I'd only recommend that strategy for a handful of people. Using your current income to fund your real estate investments is the most common path I've seen people take when they first start investing. It allows you to take baby steps while you learn and grow to achieve the goal of multiple income streams in real estate. Eventually you may quit your job, or you may not. If you get to a place where you earn enough from real estate to take care of you and your family, then you have the freedom to decide if you want to quit your job or not.

For example, I have a friend who grew up poor in Cleveland. He worked for over twenty years in the meat department at a local grocery store all while using his W-2 income to grow a portfolio of over seventy investment properties, and he is only in his 50s. Now he's retired, and when Cleveland winter hits in September (those from the Midwest understand my humor here), he chooses his city of choice to escape to and live and relax for the season, enjoying the fruits of his labor poolside under the sun.

You'll notice, my friend didn't leave his job until many years later after he built his empire. He created the wealth and freedom that allowed him to live life on his own terms. But maybe your goal is to not work a job until you retire. Do your calculations so you know exactly how much you will need to bring in from real estate before you can turn in your resignation letter. A general rule of thumb is to take the number of properties you have, divide by two, then multiply by one thousand to calculate your monthly gross income:

(#homes/2) x 1000 = gross monthly income

For example, if you own twenty homes in the urban real estate market, it would generally yield you about $10,000 per month. If that's enough for you to take care of you and your family, you now have the freedom to decide if you want to quit your job or not.

Please understand that leaving your job doesn't mean the work ends there. I see too many investors take a lackadaisical approach and think they can lay back and, like magic, their investment makes money while they sleep. Yes, that will be the case at some point, but not in the beginning. And the more homes you acquire, the more work you will have to put in until your processes are efficient and have been mastered and you have a truly passive investment. Due diligence is the key, which I'll talk more about in the next chapter.

It all starts with your mind and knowing your worth and potential and exactly what you want. As I write this book, I'm reading a book called *Atomic Habits* by James Clear. In it, he says it is in our human nature to take the path of least resistance. We don't really want to work. We only do so because we have to. Owning a real estate portfolio is the path of least resistance. I can assure you there's pleasure in not spending forty hours of your week doing something you don't like to do. If you love your job, you can continue doing that by all means. But the goal is to not settle at anything you do and to want more.

SUMMARY

Real estate investing does not have to be a huge gamble. There are people everywhere around the world investing every day. It's a realistic goal and can be done. What sets many investors and non-investors apart is taking that first step. The first step is believing in yourself and believing that it can be done. It all starts with your mindset, a goal, and knowing your why. Having a strong "why" will keep you from giving up. Like anything you've ever set out to achieve, it's a process. Whether that's getting a degree or learning a new language, it's all a process with steps you need to take to get where you want to go. There's no reason six months from now you can't achieve at least one of your investment goals. Real estate is not a get-rich-quick scheme. It will be your mindset, positive attitude, and reason for investing in the first place that will drive you past every obstacle or challenge.

Anything worth having will require hard work, commitment, and engagement. Real estate investing can open many doors of opportunity for you. You can decide to go all-in or keep another source of income as you grow. With real estate, you have options. You create the vision for your life. The only things stopping you are the limitations you put on yourself and the excuses you use to validate them.

CHAPTER THREE

Due Diligence

You must do your due diligence if you are considering investing in the urban real estate market. This is worth repeating. You must do your due diligence if you are considering investing in the urban real estate market. If there is one part where you should pay the most attention and have at least one takeaway from this book, this is it—so listen up. Lack of due diligence is where most investors fail before they even get started. Some investors don't want to put in the time upfront, or don't even know what should be done upfront, and it often costs them big time in the end. Due diligence is such an important part of the purchase process, and I've found that it is often overlooked, neglected, or done half ass. When you don't do your proper due diligence, it can either make or break you.

There is a lot that goes into analyzing, financing, and managing an investment property. You must also know how to work well with the tenants who will rent your property and how to relate with the team you will be working with to manage your property.

I've worked with a myriad of investor clients over the years, and I've been able to observe them and their behaviors. I've narrowed down these investors into three personality types.

THREE KINDS OF INVESTORS

In all my years of experience, I have met all kinds of investors, but I have morphed them into three: the overthinker, the know-it-all, and the wise investor.

The Overthinker

This kind of investor will require everything to be explained repeatedly. He will seek advice and opinions from everyone. He will spend hours and hours researching but will find it very hard to decide what he wants to do, often due to analysis paralysis, being overwhelmed with too much information, or just plain old fear. The overthinker rarely makes a move; he rarely gets to accomplish anything because he thinks too much. He also tends to be more risk adverse. His decisions are often based on emotion, and his fear keeps him from achieving financial freedom. He often misses out on prime opportunities because he waited too long to capture them or his overthinking nature caused him to pass on them.

The Know-it-All

This kind of investor usually already has some experience and success in real estate investing. He may have several properties, but this is his first time investing in the urban real estate market. He can come across as pretentious because of his investing track record and often does not take the advice of experts or take the time to do his research when entering new markets. He thinks his template for real estate investing in non-urban real estate markets can be placed right on top of the urban market and all things will be equal—but he is sadly mistaken because, as I have shown you, these two markets are vastly different.

He is the opposite of the overthinker because he won't do his due diligence. He fails to humble himself enough to ask all the necessary questions, to learn or seek advice. He fails to build relationships or network because he thinks he knows what he is doing.

The Wise Investor

This kind of investor is willing to learn and take calculated risks. He is willing to put in the work, to do his due diligence by researching the urban real estate market and its different assets. He will survive the crazy nuances of this market because he has set reasonable expectations and understands this type of investment is long term. He takes the advice of the experts around him, such as his real estate agent and property manager. He is a doer. He doesn't over-obsess or spend too much time cross-checking his investment strategy. Instead, he gathers the appropriate knowledge, trusts his gut, sets a goal, executes it, and forges ahead.

Think of which kind of investor you believe you are. Or maybe which one you may have thought you were and which one you really are. As we continue along in this chapter, we'll see how different scenarios typically play out depending on which kind of investor you are.

DO YOUR INDUSTRY RESEARCH

When it comes to due diligence, the first thing is to do your industry research. Many investors in the urban real estate market have no clue what they are getting into. I have found most live on the east or west coast or out of country, and they are blinded by the shining low prices that urban real estate housing has to offer. As a result, they make moves too quickly. For instance, a turnkey investment property in the city of Cleveland may only cost $75,000 to purchase, whereas the same property in the Bay Area or D.C. would cost $750,000 or more to purchase. But all that glitters isn't gold, and you have to take the time to determine if what you are buying is a true gem or a lemon.

I have also found that buying investment property for novice investors has become quite trendy over the years, especially with the onset of social media. A lot more people want to invest in real estate because it's the cool thing to do. There are many clichéd Instagram posts with people bragging about their accomplishments, attempting to sound like they know what they are doing, when in reality they aren't as successful as they portray themselves to be. It's easy to stand in front a rehabbed house and look like you know what you're talking about. It's easy to put on an expensive suit, regurgitate some basic knowledge, and present yourself as a real estate guru. That rehabbed house may be losing money. That guy in the nice suit may be on the brink of going bankrupt. People often tout the highlights and leave out the hardships and challenges they faced, leading potential investors to believe it's really easy to invest. When it comes to social media, focus more on the value of the content and less on the image of the person.

I could compare real estate to cryptocurrency in these times. Cryptocurrency is in high demand right now, with a lot of curiosity surrounding it. That market is moving fast, and everyone wants to get in on it. People think they can read a couple of books and be ready to buy NFTs, but many don't have a full understanding of what NFTs are or how cryptocurrency works. They just jump right in.

I've seen far too many investors in the urban real estate market get taken advantage of when they rely solely on other people's research and due diligence. Some may only consider a general property analysis they were given, for example, as sufficient before making a buying decision—without taking any steps of their own to learn about the property. The analysis may have told them it is an up and coming area when in fact it is not, or that the rent they could get from the property is "X" when really it's 30% less than that amount. The point is, take the information you are given and fact check it yourself. Even if you are paying cash, it's not a bad idea to get your own independent appraisal. Have a local real estate agent who knows the area well and can prove they have bought and sold a number of properties there run a comparative analysis. Do a Google search and read local articles and blogs about the area and what's going on there. There are a lot of people who won't have your best interest at heart simply because their interest in the property is simply the money it will make them from the sale. Once that deal is completed, you'll be left on your own to face the realities of your decisions, whether good or bad. Rely on your own research, in addition to theirs, to get a full picture before making any decisions to purchase.

I've also worked with a lot of investors who have spent thousands of dollars attending Vegas conventions on real estate and learning how to set up a self-directed IRA to purchase a number of properties (I'll talk more about this in the finance chapter), all while trusting the convention host's information without taking the time to do their own research. These investors tend to be the most hands-off because they look at this investment purely as they would a stock or mutual fund. They think they can just hire a property management company, sit back, and rake in the return on their investment. This approach can be detrimental because it gives a false sense that real estate in the urban market can simply be considered an annuity without any other work involved. Inevitably, these same investors buy properties way over market value and were told these properties were turnkey when really they were lipstick rehabs (light cosmetic work to make it look pretty without addressing any major repairs), and I find they run into many challenges a year or so later. It all becomes too much for them to handle because the cost of repairs is high or a tenant stops paying and they want out. They sell, but at a loss, and then the next uneducated investor comes along and the process repeats itself.

Real estate investments come with inherent risks; things that will throw you off balance *will* happen, so you must be prepared. There's a lot of work that comes with owning assets, and you will be responsible for some of that work; your property management company cannot take care of everything for you. You must put in the time to learn about real estate.

Across America every day, there are kids in PE class playing basketball. The teacher is friendly, the rules are relaxed, everyone gets a turn, and everyone gets a trophy. And then outside of the gym, right down the street, you've got the tough-nosed playground. This is where the players come to compete fiercely. You've got hecklers, bullies, and spectators on the sidelines looking on. On the playground, the fouls are harder and sometimes the rules are made up as you go. Bloody lips and scraped elbows are rites of passage. Right now, you're that student in gym class learning the fundamentals, but I want to turn you into a ferocious jock that everyone respects when he steps on the asphalt. Battle-tested and confident, he commands everyone's respect. The urban real estate market is a tough one, and I need to prepare you to shine.

There are a few simple things you can do starting today to learn more about real estate and the urban market. You'll want to focus about 40–50 hours on literary, digital, and firsthand research. That's it. That's equivalent to a typical work week, and this research will prepare you to take the next step.

For literary research, read no less than three books regarding real estate investing in the niche you desire to be in. Whether your goal is Airbnb properties, fix and flips, apartment buildings, or single-family residential homes, choose your focus to gain the most benefit. I highly recommend the book *How to Invest in Real Estate: The Ultimate Beginner's Guide to Getting Started* by Brandon Turner and Joshua Dorkin. It's a great book for any new investor and will introduce you to many aspects of the real estate world if you're not sure of your specific niche just yet. This very book you are reading right now can be considered a suitable resource as well and another check mark toward your reading goal.

Digital research includes podcasts, YouTube videos, and social media. In this day and age, your library is digital media. There is a wealth of knowledge to be gained by listening to conversations and other people's experiences. I recommend checking out "Bigger Pockets" real estate podcast as a great starting point.

I always encourage people, especially those investing out of state for the first time, to learn the basics of home improvement—how to replace a toilet or a furnace filter, how to lay a floor, what an updated electrical panel looks like, etc. This is all part of your firsthand research. That's valuable information because, as a homeowner, you should know or have some idea how to fix most things, whether you do it yourself or simply don't want to get taken advantage of if you hire the work out.

It's like when you take your car to the mechanic, and they start talking about different parts and systems in your car and what's wrong. We've all been there. A lot of us just nod our heads as words like carburetor, alternator, and caliper are casually used by the mechanic; meanwhile, you have no clue what they are talking about. However, if you had some familiarity with cars, how they work, and the terminology, you'd have a better understanding of what the issues are with your car and what really needs to be done to fix it or what could wait.

I remember the days when you could go to Home Depot and take elementary-level classes for free to learn all sorts of things about home improvement. Nowadays, you can YouTube just about anything to get a good grasp on the ins and outs of the inner workings of a house.

It's also helpful to know the general prices of materials and labor for most home projects. While you're not expected to be an expert, general knowledge is key. How much is it to replace a hot water heater? To replace a roof? Gather this information and keep notes on your phone or in a notebook for quick reference.

Firsthand research also includes mentorship. Mentorship is priceless and can come in many different forms. Do you recall when I mentioned my friend from college who introduced me to real estate? Without his guidance, I would have never bought my first investment property. I would tag along with him as he viewed properties he was considering buying, and I would also be there when he met with his contractors to discuss the scope of work needed for a rehab. I learned so much from those experiences. I have found it extremely important to have someone you trust who can help guide you, show you the ropes, and give you valuable tools to navigate this real estate game. Your literary and digital research is important but will only take you so far. There's nothing like getting into the trenches—that's where the real learning happens.

Finding a mentor can sound daunting, and you might be saying "Where the hell do I start?" Simply put, start with the closest people to you—your friends and family. Some people may say, "But Byron, I don't know anyone in real estate." And to that I challenge you to think bigger. Let your friends and family know you are interested in getting into real estate investing. Let them know you are looking for someone to learn from. Perhaps someone in your family is already investing and would be happy to mentor you. If there's no one in your immediate circle, your friends and family may know of a co-worker, one of their friends, or someone at church. Don't limit your beliefs as to how large your circle can expand when you reach out to the people you know.

After you've started with the people you know, I suggest joining local real estate investing groups. Nearly every city has a few of them. Google "Real Estate Investment Association" (REIA). This is a popular organization that has local chapters scattered across the nation, and they usually meet monthly. You'll have the opportunity to meet a variety of people in the industry—contractors, real estate agents, insurance agents, different types of lenders, and other investors. By being a part of REIA, I found the eviction attorney we have now worked with for years. Many chapters have meetings open to anyone, but if you pay to join and become a member, you'll receive added benefits. I highly encourage going this route because REIA also offers a number of trainings. You'll be able to talk with and learn from other investors, and it's a great way to identify a mentor.

You can also Google local real estate meet up groups. These groups tend to be less formal but are just as valuable. I guarantee there are other investors in your area who want to learn from each other and share advice and resources. I consider this a form of mentorship. Many of these groups focus on specific areas of real estate investing, which gives you a chance to hone your skills in a specific niche.

Social media is another incredible resource. It may be tempting to reach out to one of the top gurus in the industry and ask for a few minutes of their time to pick their brain; but you'll find they are often so busy, they either won't have the time, or they'll charge for their time. Instead, start with someone local to the area you want to invest in. The person doesn't have to be a big name. It can simply be someone who's content you like, who posts on a consistent basis, and who you connect with. If you don't know where to start, search hashtags like #realestateinvesting, #buyandholdrealestateinvesting, or better yet, add a city name like #clevelandrealestateinvesting or #memphisrealestateinvesting. See who shows up. Take a look at their pages and follow the ones you like. After you've gotten a good feel for their content, send a direct message asking for fifteen minutes on their calendar to discuss their real estate investing experience. If they oblige, make sure you have five or so of your top questions written down and ready to ask. Make the most use of the opportunity. Not everyone will make themselves available, but you may be surprised at how many will. This doesn't have to turn into a full mentorship. It may be the one conversation you have, but you get answers to your questions and can continue to follow and engage with their content.

Always approach learning from others and finding a mentor from a place of humility. Being humble and a strong listener will take you far. And understand that the more time and energy you put into mastering real estate investing, the more you will get out of it.

Let's take it back to our three kinds of investors. Industry research is where the Overthinker gets stuck. They overdo it and can never have enough information or do enough research, and they often don't get past this step. The Know-it-All and the Wise Investor will usually navigate past this phase and on to the next with little problem.

DO YOUR MARKET RESEARCH

Think of industry research as taking a look at the market while in an airplane 30,000 feet up in the air. From this view, you'll get a good grasp of the market as a whole. When it comes to market research, think of looking at the market from a drone view. You're still getting an overall picture from above, but more drilled down and specific to an area.

The first place to start your market research is by vetting two of the most important members of your team—your real estate agent and property manager.

Work with a licensed real estate agent who can not only help you identify properties that you might be interested in, but who can also help you learn the area, average rent rates, and comparable sales, as well as connect you with other resources like contractors or inspectors. Real estate agents sometimes have access to off-market properties as well. These are properties that are available but not publicly listed for sale. They could also be listings that may be coming soon to the market that an agent will have prior knowledge of.

Remember, real estate agents are licensed professionals, and you should treat them as such. They have taken classes and tests to obtain their license, and they take continuing education classes to maintain it. They know more than the average person when it comes to real estate and how it works. They are held to a higher standard and a code of ethics. Treat them with respect and be respectful of their time.

There are a few ways I identify a good real estate agent to work with. Make sure to vet at least two to three agents before you make your decision. The right agent should have strong knowledge and experience in the urban real estate market and be able to navigate its complexities well. This is important. Not all agents are created equal when it comes to the urban market. Choose wisely. The first and easiest way to find a real estate agent that meets this criteria is to look up homes currently listed for sale in the zip codes you want to focus on. If you see that quite a few are listed by the same agent or agents, reach out to them to learn more. This means they are already doing business in the area, have had at least one or more other people trust them enough to hire them, and they will more than likely have a good understanding of the area. Give those agents a call. Search their profile on Zillow, and you'll be able to see all of the properties they have sold within the last twelve months. This will let you see which cities and areas the majority of their sales are in. The agents will likely know these areas well enough to be familiar with their distinct characteristics and can help you highlight the hidden gems that outsiders may deem as undesirable. Lastly, check their Zillow and Google reviews. Do the agents have just a couple or many? This can be telling as well.

You may also want to consider an agent who is newer to real estate (has been selling for two to three years). Sometimes the top agents are very busy, and you may not get the personalized attention you are seeking—a newer agent is often hungry. This was me when I first started. My first investor client took a chance on me when I was just a few months into the business. I had the energy and excitement to learn the market, and I was willing to go above and beyond. That investor loved my passion, and we ended up working together over several years during which I helped him purchase several hundred homes. Keep in mind newer agents are often mentored by top agents and have access to the same resources and can get help when needed. They aren't completely on an island, so don't assume you won't get the same level of service as from an experienced agent. You may have to be a little more patient, but it could work well in your favor.

The next person for your team is your property manager or management company. I have an entire chapter dedicated to this so I won't go into too much detail here, but know that they, along with your real estate agent, will be your best friends in investing. Get a referral from your real estate agent for a good property manager, and if your agent is well versed in the area, they will likely have a couple of names for you. If they don't, a simple Google search will provide several to choose from. When it comes to the urban real estate market, it's critical to find a manager or management company familiar with and willing to work in the area. You might find that a company is one of the top in the city; however, they only manage A&B properties. You need to know this upfront.

One huge piece of market research that I see many investors fail to do, particularly those purchasing properties who live out of state and out of the country, is not physically viewing the property prior to purchase. I've seen it happen far too many times—they've relied on a video, photos, or statistics they found online without actually seeing the property for themselves, and they get burned. And every now and then, I come across investors who purchased without seeing the property AT ALL. Can you believe that?

As you become a more savvy investor and familiar with the urban market, seeing the property in person isn't always necessary. However, for your first few purchases, I highly recommend spending the money and time to see firsthand what you are buying. Walk the streets. Smell the air. Those few hundred dollars you'll spend on a flight could save you thousands down the road when you see that the house itself isn't bad but the majority of homes on the street are boarded up. Or the street looks good, but the house doesn't quite add up to what the photos on Zillow look like. I see it happen time and time again. Investors make bad purchases and are stuck.

Taking a trip into town does not have to be costly. Let's conservatively estimate (depending on how many people are traveling with you) an early morning red eye flight at $400, rental car at $100, and food at $100. Just consider that $600 part of your investment. Before you get to town, schedule appointments with your real estate agent to see the properties you are interested in. Ask the agent to show you around different areas of town when you arrive. Make time to connect with any property managers you've vetted as well. By planning ahead, you should be able to accomplish all of this, grab a bite to eat, and be back on a plane home all in one day. Making the trip into town also shows your real estate agent how serious you are. The worst thing people often do is waste an agent's time. When you come prepared and ready, your agent will recognize and appreciate this.

This is a good place to remind you of our Know-it-All Investor. When it comes to market research, they usually aren't going to do their due diligence in the market, won't come in to town to see the properties they are buying, and typically won't use a real estate agent or vet their property manager. If they do use an agent, they are more likely to just use them as their virtual tour guide and less as a resource.

DO YOUR ASSET RESEARCH

Asset research is doing your due diligence to learn as much as you can about the property itself. You'd be surprised how many people buy a property without learning whether it is a single family or multi-family, or even whether it's vacant or occupied. I told you, I've seen just about everything. Asset research should involve knowing what the property values are in the area, what the taxes are, and if any taxes are unpaid. Get financials from the seller for the property going back at least twelve months that outline all of the expenses they incurred (utilities, landscaping, repairs, work orders, etc.). If the property is currently managed by a management company, this should be easy for a seller to provide. Some sellers may not be as organized and may have limited information, but you'll at least want to make sure you request it. Learn about the tenants, and ask for a copy of rent rolls, leases, and tenant ledgers to see if they are current with rent. Don't just take a seller's word for it.

You'll also want to go to the county auditor's website and look up the property. This will provide a wealth of information. Here you can see if there are any back taxes owed, any city assessments that are paid as part of the taxes, and you should be able to confirm bedroom count, unit count, square footage, etc. You can also see how many times the property had been bought and sold over the years. If there are several transfers, this may indicate there have been problems with the property. If there have only been one or two over a long period of time, this may indicate the seller will be more familiar with the property and they've had fewer problems. There may also be websites where you can check whether any permits have been pulled so you know if any additions or rehabs that were completed were inspected by the city. Verify the property isn't on the city's condemned list. Your agent should be able to assist with getting this information, as well as any title company or real estate attorney. Find out as much as you can to make an educated decision when it comes time to place an offer.

For novice and first time investors, I always encourage buying a turnkey, rent-ready property or one that is already cash-flowing. I find too often that many investors romanticize renovating a property thanks to our friends at HGTV who make it looks so fun and easy. The idea sounds great. Buy a property below market value, and rehab it to potentially yield a better return. The reality is, full rehabs should be reserved for investors who have a few of them under their belts. It's often difficult, especially in the urban market, to find good, reliable contractors who will do quality work. You'll find yourself having to micromanage the work, and this comes with even greater difficulty if you do not live locally. Homes with no work needed or needing just minor cosmetic improvements are ideal and what you should initially seek to purchase. Set yourself up for a quick victory when you start investing by buying a turnkey property. You can get up and running quickly and start making money faster with fewer headaches. The better this first purchase goes, the more likely you'll want to continue investing.

Once you are under contract, you are afforded the opportunity to do a full home inspection. This is a step you don't want to skip as a new investor. I do see more savvy investors get by with just sending their contractor to do a walk through to assess needed repairs and estimate the associated costs. Their goal in those cases isn't necessarily to review every nook and cranny, but rather to see how much it'll cost to get the property rent ready and the time it will take. This will be your goal as well, but if you are a rookie to investing, hire a licensed home inspector to thoroughly assess the property and provide you with a written report. This will also help you learn more about the property and add to your asset research.

When you have a professional home inspection, they are going to tell you all the details regarding the property. You'll learn about which repairs may need immediate action and which can be deferred. You'll also get a good idea of the age of the roof and the mechanicals, as well as their condition.

A good investor is able to decipher an inspection report and not get too concerned or alarmed about every little item the inspector adds to it. This relates back to industry research and why it's so valuable to have a good understanding of the inner workings of a home.

What you'll mainly want to consider from the inspection report when determining whether or not to move forward with the purchase are these five things:

1. Electrical

2. Plumbing
3. Foundation
4. HVAC
5. Roof

These are the systems of the property you'll want to pay the most attention to. Is the electrical updated, or is there old knob and tube wiring that you'll likely be forced to update once you start doing any kitchen or bath renovations? Is the plumbing old copper plumbing or is it CPVC? Are there any major cracks or shifts in the foundation? Is the basement dry, or is there excessive moisture and dampness? Through your asset and market research and assistance from your agent, you'll be able to discern what is typical for similar properties in the area and what should give you pause. Have a budget in mind for necessary repairs identified in these top areas so you can quickly assess whether or not this is a practical and possible investment.

Now, I'm not saying the other items listed in a report won't be of value to you, but just understand they will likely be minor and should not hold as much weight as the top five listed above.

Let's sum this all up and refer back to our three Investors. We are typically left with one investor type by the end of this phase and that's the Wise Investor. They follow all of the steps I've outlined and are the prime example of how to dominate during the due diligence phase of investing.

SUMMARY

Due diligence won't completely absolve you from having problems when investing in real estate, but when done properly and fully, you can certainly minimize issues and set yourself up for success. There are certain risks that come with investing in the urban market. It is your job to educate yourself about these risks to mitigate them as much as possible.

Industry research will give you a high-level overview and should include digital, literary, and firsthand. Market research will include a more in-depth process that involves building your team and getting to know the ins and outs of the market and properties you're considering. When at all possible, put eyes on the properties you are buying and have them inspected. The final phase, asset research, will put you in the best position to understand what you're purchasing. Remember, identify a mentor to guide you and teach you the ropes; this will be invaluable as you learn and grow your portfolio. There are three types of investors—the Overthinker, the Know-it-All, and the Wise Investor. Becoming a Wise Investor will yield you the most success as you continue your investment journey.

CHAPTER FOUR

Financing

I often find many people are gung-ho about investing in real estate when they are first introduced to the idea. They quickly grasp and understand that it can provide an additional revenue stream, tax benefits, and help to build generational wealth. But when I ask many people why they aren't currently investing, the number one reason is finances. They either don't have enough money, credit, or resources to acquire the needed money. **Don't allow a perceived lack of finances to be your reason for not pursing real estate investment.** In this chapter, we'll explore multiple options for financing purchases to help you choose the ones that best suit you. This won't be an exhaustive list, but rather a good starting point to give you basic knowledge. I suggest you extend your research past this book and do a deeper dive into the methods that interest you most.

Traditional Financing

You've likely heard of all sorts of creative financing that can be done to invest in real estate, but for some it's as simple as starting with the basics. No need to make it complicated.

Traditional financing includes obtaining a mortgage loan though a bank or mortgage lender. These are your standard conventional loans similar to those used when purchasing a primary property except the terms are usually different for investors versus owner occupants.

Banks are going to be very strict and run a tight ship, so be prepared to have all of your ducks in a row. Gone are the days where you could get a loan without providing any documentation whatsoever, or by stating what your income is without it being verified. Yes, this was really a thing. As an investor, you will be expected to put at least 20% down for a single-family and 25%–30% or more for multi-family homes, up to four units (more than four units is considered a commercial property, and I will be discussing residential financing options here). The only way, as an investor, you can qualify to put down less than 20% is if you plan to occupy one of the units. This strategy has become affectionately known over the years in the real estate world as house hacking. This is where you live in one unit and rent out the others so your rents cover your housing expenses. I absolutely love this strategy for first-time home buyers who are willing to forego the traditional first home and turn their first major life purchase into a money-generating asset that can help fund their dream home. If the urban real estate market isn't your location of choice, then house hacking likely won't be the way to go.

The bank will also require you to provide W2s, tax returns, bank statements, and a list of your current assets and debts. Most of the time you'll need to have a credit score of 620 or higher. Of course, the higher the better. Investors also typically pay a higher interest rate or lenders may assess additional investor-related fees. The loan will go through traditional underwriting where it will feel like they've stripped you down and combed every inch of your body to make sure you are suitable to acquire a home loan with minimal risk of defaulting.

Traditional financing is a good route for those who have good credit and some cash on hand. It's a way to leverage your funds across multiple properties instead of pooling all of your funds into buying one property all in cash. The down side is for those who don't have a lot of cash on hand, where a 20% down payment may be a challenge depending on what price point you're at. As I mentioned, if you don't have good credit or all your paperwork in order, traditional financing can be intimidating, a bit of a hassle, or often not the best option for some people.

401(k) Accounts

A 401(k) account is a type of retirement account offered through an employer. There are various types depending on whether you work at a for-profit or non-profit company, but for the sake of keeping things simple, I'll refer to them all as 401(k)s. In general, they all work the same way. You're investing your money, pre-tax, into a mix of stocks and bonds which usually include stock for the company you work for, if they are publicly traded. Your employer will often match you dollar for dollar up to a certain amount. Over the last several decades, we've seen pensions reach extinction as 401(k)s rolled in and people enjoyed being able to essentially double their investment by using the company match to accelerate their dividends.

The downside to a 401(k) is that the money invested is meant to be saved for retirement and cannot be withdrawn before the age of 59-1/2 without facing huge penalties. There is one exception to this rule, however, and that is if you plan to withdraw the money to purchase a home. In this case, you are able to borrow money from your account and pay yourself back, through future paychecks, with interest. You do not pay penalties or taxes. You do lose the opportunity for your money to grow in your account during this time, but the benefit of using it to buy an income-producing property tends to outweigh that loss. And for many, investing that money in real estate—instead of in preselected mutual funds in your 401(k) that you have no control over—is a better bet. Every plan is different, so you'll want to make sure you check the rules regarding your particular plan, and consult with your financial advisor before you proceed.

Self-Directed IRAs

A Self-Directed IRA (SDIRA) is another retirement vehicle that can be used to purchase real estate. It's just like a traditional or Roth IRA in that it allows tax advantages and has the same contribution limits. The main difference is that more traditional IRAs invest in stocks and bonds, whereas with SDIRAs, you can diversify your investments into things like real estate and nontraded businesses.

To buy and own property via your IRA, you will need a custodian—an entity specializing in self-directed accounts that will manage the transaction, associated paperwork, and financial reporting. Everything goes through the custodian to keep you from violating the various rules regarding this type of retirement plan. It's still important to know all the rules though, because a violation can mean your entire account is at stake, and you could end up having to pay income tax. This plan will also require a property management company to manage the properties within it. Any expenses required for the property can be paid out through the plan, but all gains must go back into the plan. They cannot be pocketed.

The pros of SDIRAs are you often get higher returns on your money, and you can diversify your investments. It's a good idea to have a financial advisor well versed in SDIRAs to help you navigate the complexities. The cons of SDIRAs are there are a lot of rules to follow, you tend to pay higher fees, and the money is not liquid since all your gains are directed back into your account. Always consult your financial planner or accountant when considering this option.

Whole Life Insurance

Securing a life insurance policy doesn't only provide you coverage in case tragedy strikes; it can also be a great avenue for investing. There are two different types of life insurance. There's term life insurance and whole/permanent life insurance. With term, you pay a premium each month for a policy that will pay out a certain amount to your beneficiaries upon your death. With whole life insurance, you not only pay a premium that provides the same benefit, but you're also able to add money on top of that premium that gets invested into stocks and bonds. This cash value that grows inside your policy can be withdrawn at any time, no matter your age and without penalty. Whole life insurance policies make great tax shelters for your money as well. For those of you who quickly max out your annual retirement contributions each year with your other plans, investing your money in a whole life policy can yield similar tax benefits.

Whole life insurance policies can be a nice source of funds for your real estate purchases, but there is a downside to them as well. One con to whole life insurance is that the premiums are typically higher than term policies, and you will pay monthly premiums for the entire duration of your life instead of a fixed amount of time. Therefore, if you don't plan to use the cash value benefits, getting a term policy for basic life insurance coverage may make more sense. It can also take some time to build your cash value, and it's important to consistently invest in the policy monthly to see the most rate of return. Identify an insurance agent who can help you determine which strategy is best for your needs, and who can best advise regarding tax benefits.

Personal Credit

The use of personal credit to finance real estate transactions has become somewhat popular over the years. It's a bit riskier, so I don't recommend this route for everyone. Credit card interest rates are notoriously high, often between 15% and 25%. If you don't pay off your balance each month, you could end up buried under a mountain of debt. This is why I suggest only using this method of financing when you're able to secure an introductory 0% interest credit card for at least a period of 12 to 24 months. You typically need superb credit to qualify for these offers.

So, how does it work? You can either search online for 0% interest credit cards and apply for one, or you can utilize a card that you already have. If it's a card you have, contact the credit card company to see if they are offering any 0% balance transfers. If your card has a low balance and plenty of available credit, you can ask the card company if you qualify to have new purchases at 0% interest. If so, most credit card companies will send you blank checks to make purchases using your available credit. You can then write a check to yourself, and deposit the cash into your account.

This method can be risky, and you must have an exit strategy. Because I encourage investors in the urban real estate market to buy and hold their properties, this is not meant to be a long-term financing option. You'll want to make sure you get the 0% interest rate, or a rate as low as possible, locked in for the longest amount of time possible so you are able to pay down your card. Make sure you maintain good credit, because if you do not pay down that card before the promotional period is up, your best bet is to transfer the remaining balance to another 0% card. In theory, you could continue to do this until the entire balance is paid, but be prepared to start paying interest on the remaining balance if you're not able to pay it off or transfer it in time. This is where people can get in trouble. When that promotional period ends, the higher rates can make paying off the balance a lot more challenging. This may be a better option when you're looking for cash to fund repairs, turnovers, or rehabs.

However, this method can work well for those who have great credit to leverage, are organized, and can keep up with monthly payments to avoid losing the promotional rate. This method is not ideal for those who are not good with their money, who don't have great credit, and who are not organized.

Business Credit

Building business credit is similar to building personal credit; however, think of it as playing the same game but on a different field with different rules. With business credit, you can often obtain much higher lines of credit, and you're able to keep it separate from your personal credit. I'm not an attorney or accountant, but you'll want to consult with one to help establish a business entity. There are several options, but a popular one is a limited liability corporation (LLC). Once you have your business entity, it could take as little as three to six months to build your credit to where you'll be able to secure credit cards with $30,000 or even $100,000+ limits at 0% rates. Like with your personal credit, these 0% interest rates are short term, promotional rates so you'll need a plan as to how you'll pay that money back in a short amount of time. I see many investors using business credit for fix and flips rather than buy and holds for that reason. There is a specific way to go about building business credit. There are different tiers you'll need to reach by making certain purchases before you can secure those higher credit limits. There's a different credit scoring system that you'll need to be familiar with as well.

A great resource to help you establish and build business credit is Excel Capital Group. Based out of Chicago, they provide training, courses, and group sessions to business owners all over the world. Again, consult an attorney and tax professional before setting anything up in order to make the right choices for your particular situation.

Hard Money Loan

A hard money loan is geared toward people who are not able to qualify for traditional financing. The money comes from companies who are licensed and experienced. Their criteria for lending is not as strict as a bank or mortgage company, which makes them attractive. With a hard money loan, the property you purchase is used as collateral. The value of the property is used to determine your loan amount and interest rate.

I absolutely do not recommend a hard money loan unless you are a more experienced, savvy investor with a high risk tolerance. It may be a fast and less stringent way to borrow money, but it is very expensive. It comes with high-interest rates and fees. They typically don't embody favorable terms, nor do they give you enough time to make your money back—only three to six months, twelve if you're lucky. As I've advised, a buy-and-hold strategy is most ideal in the urban market, and hard money is not meant for long term investments. Make sure to tread lightly when considering this option.

Private Money Lending

Private money lending can be one person or a group of people who have their own personal money to lend and who determine their own terms. It can be anyone really, and they typically aren't regulated or governed by any established rules. Just as I explained regarding searching for a mentor, starting with your friends and family to seek a loan is an option you don't want to shy away from. You never know who may be willing to help or invest with you. There are also private businesses who may provide private loans as well.

Another option to consider is partnering with a group of people to pool your money together. Clearly define each person's role. Who will be active investors with a say in the decisions made? Will some prefer to be silent investors, content to invest, sit back, and wait for their return? Will you create a business everyone has ownership in that will be used to purchase property? How will everything be split? All these terms and more should be discussed and determined ahead of time. Having an attorney draft an official agreement will help minimize any future confusion or misunderstandings.

The pros of private money lending are it's a lot less formal than traditional financing so there are fewer guidelines and pre-qualifications, and oftentimes credit is not used to determine eligibility. The cons of private money lending are you will generally pay more in interest and fees, and if you are working with friends and family, relationships can become strained if the investment goes south.

Seller Financing

Seller financing is an option many people don't even realize is an option. With traditional financing, you obtain a mortgage from the bank. With seller financing, the seller essentially becomes the bank, and you, as the buyer, draft an agreement directly with them to finance the purchase of their property. Sometimes you're able to negotiate a smaller down payment (unlike the 20% minimums with a bank) and a reasonable interest rate. Once the sale is final, you become the owner of the property and responsible for everything—taxes, insurance, maintenance, etc.—just as you would with any purchase. You then pay your monthly mortgage payments to the seller, now lender. I would advise you to have the paperwork drawn up by an attorney, with a written agreement outlining the interest rate, schedule of payments, and the consequences if you default.

Most seller financing loans are amortized over 20 or 30 years, allowing your payments to stay low, but with a five-year term ending in a balloon payment. A balloon payment is when the entire remainder of the loan is due at the end of the loan term. For example, you may have a loan for $65,000 with a down payment of $10,000 and a balloon payment due after five years. This means that in five years, if you've only paid down $5,000 of the $55,000 financed, you'll owe the seller/lender the entire $50,000 balance. Many investors choose to refinance their loan with a traditional bank before the balloon payment is due. Refinancing tends to be easier than getting a brand new loan.

The pros of seller financing are being able to get a home loan with a lower down payment and essentially little to no pre-qualification for the loan, unlike with traditional financing. The cons are that it can be challenging to find a seller willing to participate, and you need to be prepared with an exit strategy or you could be left with a large sum to pay back in a few years.

THE 'BRRR' METHOD

The BRRR Method is short for the Buy, Rehab, Rent, and Refinance method. You purchase a property, preferably below market value, rehab it, and rent it out. The goal is that after the renovations are complete, the new value for the home is high enough that you are able to refinance with enough cash equity to purchase another property and repeat the process.

This method is great because you are able to use your first purchase to finance future purchases. In addition, you're building your portfolio of income properties that can produce a nice residual with relatively low upfront cost. The downside is that you'll still need to determine how you'll finance or pay cash for the initial investment. Several of the other methods I've mentioned already could be considered.

The BRRR Method is typically best used in A&B markets and can be more challenging in most urban real estate markets. This is because most home values in the urban market are lower with not much appreciation, especially fast appreciation. When you go to refinance, the bank may not be able to do a cash out refinance because there won't be enough equity in the property. If you do try this method, there are a lot of variables to consider, such as how much you purchased the property for and how low you're able to keep your rehab costs. I'm not saying it absolutely cannot work in the urban real estate market, but the BRRR Method is not ideal for this type of market. As always, run your own analysis to determine what will work best for you.

SUMMARY

Lack of finances should not be a hindrance to investing in real estate. There are many ways to get funding that include:

- Traditional Financing
- 401(k) Accounts
- Self-Directed IRAs
- Whole Life Insurance
- Personal Credit
- Business Credit
- Hard Money Lending
- Private Money Lending
- Seller Financing
- The BRRR Method

As I mentioned at the beginning of this chapter, this is not a complete guide to financing. This is meant to give you a basic understanding of the options available to help you get started. Some will work well in the urban real estate market, and some won't, such as hard money lending or personal credit which work better for flipping houses than buy and hold. I presented multiple options to consider throughout your real estate investing journey. Some options will require you to have good credit—such as traditional financing—some you'll need to have your own money, and some you'll be able to leverage other people's money. Certain methods are better for experienced investors but should be avoided by new investors, such as hard money lending. In this business, there's more than one way to skin a cat, so get familiar with them all. Remember, before you take any step toward purchasing a property, do your research and speak to your financial advisor and tax professionals to assist with developing your strategy. Run your own numbers, understand your personal risk tolerance, and do your due diligence.

CHAPTER FIVE

Tenants

Let's do a quick recap. So far you've learned the ins and outs of the urban real estate market, how to do your due diligence, and how to finance your investment—all while building your wealth and freedom mindset. Now it's time to dive in to what I consider the lifeblood of every real estate asset, the core, the soul—the tenants. In real estate investing, you'll find your tenants can be your biggest asset or your biggest liability. But you can't have a successful long-term investment without them, so it's important to learn from the start how to identify good tenants, understand the lifestyle of most urban market tenants, and how to foster good relationships with them.

Most of you will never meet, see, nor know your tenants because the majority of investors in the urban real estate market hire a property manager or management company to manage their properties. My goal in this chapter is to pull back the curtain and provide behind-the-scenes insight of how everything works. This will allow you to view your property from the lens of a property manager and give you a full understanding whether you choose to manage your own property or outsource.

UNDERSTANDING URBAN MARKET TENANTS

For many years, the relationship between tenant and landlord in the urban real estate market has been strained. Somewhere along the lines, a deep level of distrust developed to the point where it is often an us (owner) vs them (tenants) mentality. If we take a step back and look at the history of the urban real estate market, we can shed a bit of light on why this is.

If you think back to the '40s, '50s, and '60s in America, most neighborhoods were still segregated. There was a strong sense of community where everyone knew everyone and looked out for one another. Most people owned their home, and it likely had been passed down from generation to generation. As desegregation unfolded, residents in the urban areas began to move out to the suburbs. If they didn't sell their home, they would leave it to a family member or rent it to someone they knew. Overtime, this urban sprawl led to a decline in businesses, population, and tax revenue, which greatly affected schools and had a great overall economic impact. In addition, many of these areas were Rust Belt cities like Detroit, Milwaukee, and Memphis, and saw a shift as their main industries changed with major corporations exiting and many people moving out of town right behind them. More outside investors, and even local investors, came in and saw investing in this market as purely a business move with little actual investment in the community. As more properties became rentals and more investors entered the market, landlords grew a reputation of not properly caring for properties and leaving tenants to live in less than ideal conditions. Tenants often had little leverage. Landlords, in the eyes of tenants, were slumlords that cared nothing about them, only the rent check. Tenants, however, didn't always take accountability either and would not always do their part to keep properties well kept. This tug-of-war, so to speak, has dampened tenant/landlord relations. But it doesn't have to be that way. The quicker you truly understand how people in the urban market live and who they are, the quicker you'll have a good experience with your tenants.

A few things to note about tenants in the urban market are they value family, tend to be loyal to those who are loyal to them, and put their safety as a high priority. With lower economic conditions, most tenants are of lower income with tight budgets and often need some type of third-party assistance to help with paying rent and utilities. Although there is higher crime in the urban real estate market, you'll find the majority of your tenants will not be criminals. Most just want to go to work, come home to spend time with their family, and get up the next day to do it all again.

Going forward, we'll discuss how to have a good relationship with your tenants and how to keep them longer to protect your investment. I'll reveal my strategies from marketing the property and screening tenants all the way through handling maintenance requests, tenant conflicts, and evictions. I'll give firsthand accounts, from my own trial and error, and lessons learned that have allowed me to perfect my systems. This is all meant to set you on a direct path to success.

PREPARING YOUR PROPERTY

The other day, an investor told me about a property he wanted my company to market to find a tenant. He said his contractor had said all necessary work was completed, and now he was ready for the next step. My first question to him was, "Is the house rent ready?" He said, "Yes!" I then rephrased the question because I've learned that many investors don't quite understand what that means. So I asked, "Would *YOU* live there right now with how it is?" He paused and responded, "No."

Preparing your property for renting is one of the single most important things you do as an investor. When done right, you will attract a larger pool of the right tenants, and you will have fewer maintenance issues down the road. Begin with the mindset of making it a place where you would feel comfortable living. I'm not saying that if you have a high standard of living the property needs to match that, but pay attention to the things that will make a home desirable. Just because the majority of your tenants will come from low income does not mean they won't have standards of their own. For instance, it's often the little things that prospective tenants notice, things that may seem insignificant on the surface but could cause them to not rent your property. Here are some of the things I make a priority when preparing a unit for rent:

- Make sure outlets and light switches have cover plates that aren't broken or discolored.

- Make sure all of the light fixtures match and have working light bulbs.

- Have the temperature set to a comfortable level, especially in extreme heat or cold. Don't turn the utilities off. It should be a positive experience when tenants tour your property, and it won't be if they are freezing to death or sweating like crazy.

This all seems trivial but, trust me, has a major impact on a prospect's view of your property. If not done right, it sends the message of, if you don't care enough to put a cover plate over the outlet, what will happen when a major repair is needed?

The next thing to consider are updates. Tenants will typically choose a more updated property over one that's not. This simply means pay attention to current design trends. I always recommend:

- Changing the carpet or flooring if your budget allows. Again, it doesn't have to be top of the line, but new carpet will go a long way. Choose a darker gray or tan color to help hide future/inevitable stains. Avoid dark brown or white carpet. In duplexes, in particular, I recommend carpet on the second floor to help buffer noise heard on the first floor.

- Choosing nice, vinyl plank flooring for your kitchens and baths. If there are natural hardwood floors in the main living areas, consider buffing and re-staining, but don't just paint over it. It'll look cheap.

- Changing out light fixtures that look old or outdated.

- Making sure there is at least one smoke detector or carbon monoxide detector on each floor (or whatever the city code requires).

- Making sure all of the windows open and aren't painted shut and have screens.

- Making sure cabinet doors in the kitchen and baths properly open and close. Consider adding nice hardware.
- Reglazing the bathtub if it looks worn and dirty.
- Adding a fresh coat of paint, selecting neutral, modern colors. Don't skip this step. Gray is trending as of this writing.

Prospective tenants pay attention to all of these things and you should too.

The exterior is just as important as the interior, if not more. As they say, first impressions are lasting impressions. Here are my tips for the exterior:

- Make sure there's no chipping paint, especially on the front porch.
- Install handrails on steps.
- Add landscaping. Even simple landscaping can help your property standout. Mulch and a few $20 plants from a home improvement store are a great touch. I do this with my own properties, and I highly recommend it.
- Paint the front door, if needed, and make sure storm doors are in good shape; if not, replace or remove them.
- Make sure there is proper lighting near entrances and on the driveway. Tenants like to know their safety is being taken into consideration.

Most of these things don't have to be expensive. I get it, the cost can add up, but these are smart investments into your property.

MARKETING YOUR PROPERTY

Online marketing these days still reigns supreme when it comes to getting your units in front of the most people. This is one of the rare times you'll hear me promote Zillow as a great site. They allow you to easily upload your property, and most people will search Zillow first when looking for rental properties. There is also have rent.com, homes.com, craigslist, and many others.

While you can't always time when you'll need to market your properties, the first quarter of the year is usually the best time to get a good pool of tenants to choose from. It will also be the busiest. Why? Two things. One, the holidays are over and people are ready to focus on the new year; and two, people are starting to file their taxes and can use their tax return money for first month's rent and security deposit.

Don't shy away from marketing your property in the wintertime or around the end of the year. Getting a tenant in your unit the last quarter of the year can set you up nicely year after year, because tenants will be more likely to renew the lease each year rather than move around the holidays. This is especially true in markets like Cleveland, Detroit, or Indianapolis where the winters get really cold. When a lease starts and ends during the summertime, it's easier for tenants to leave as they'll usually have more options and are more willing to move when it's warm.

SCREENING TENANTS

After preparing and marketing your property, it's time to screening prospective tenants. If you are using a property management company, there should be an application process in place and a service that can pull all of the necessary information for a prospect into one report. If you are doing this on your own, you can utilize similar services like Turbo Tenant, mysmartmove.com, or rentprep.com to gather a prospect's background information. Either way, an application fee is usually charged to offset any cost to you. While screening tenants, here are the top four criteria to focus on:

1. **Criminal Record**

When screening prospects, do a check of their criminal history. In the urban market, it's important to note that it's not uncommon for a prospective tenant to have something on their criminal record. If something comes up, you'll want to ask questions to get more clarification because not all crimes are created equal. The American judicial system is funny. I can't even keep track of the number of times I've seen people with a weapons charge on their record and come to find out, when I dug deeper, that "weapon" was actually a pen or pencil. I don't consider this a real crime, and you can see how the lines can get blurred. Even marijuana possession on someone's record is not something that I, personally, count against them.

When it comes to a person's criminal record, your main goal is to determine if they pose a safety threat. If a prospect has been convicted of a homicide, sexual assault, or fraud, these are the types of crimes that, for me, would disqualify someone.

2. Credit Score

It's important to run a credit check for your prospective tenants, but many investors will be surprised to learn that credit isn't one of the screening criteria I rank high on the list. A lot of investors tell me they want their tenants to have a high credit score and be credit worthy, and I remind them that when you invest in the urban market, many people are going to have low credit scores. Those with high scores are likely to buy a home versus rent. The overall score isn't as important as what appears on the credit report itself. This gives a better picture of whether you want to rent to someone or not. Check how many accounts they have in collections; this can be an indicator of whether they keep up with their bills. A student loan or medical debt on their report I tend to let slide. If a prospective tenant has set up to have their rent and utility payments post to their credit report monthly, this may indicate they are consistent with paying their rent and utilities on time.

3. Employment and Income Verification

Employment and income verification are two of the top criteria to consider when screening tenants. Their gross monthly income should be at least three times the rent amount. If more than one adult will be on the lease, screen all adults and combine their income to verify the minimum income requirement. Consider all sources of income, and make sure they provide documentation. This can be one month's worth of pay stubs from a job, social security, alimony, child support, etc. If someone is getting subsidized rent, they'll need to show this as well. I talk more about this later on in the chapter.

Do not waiver on the income qualification. If someone does not have enough income, you are setting them and yourself up for unmet expectations later. Only consider current income; a prospect may say they are starting a new job, but you can't be certain they actually will.

Contact their current employer for verification as well. I also like to see that a tenant has been at the same place of employment for at least two years. If it's less than that or they have had several jobs in the last few of years, this can be a red flag. I also understand the nature of the urban market, and people do tend to change jobs more frequently so keep this in mind. Because people do change jobs, if you renew a tenant's lease, ask them to provide updated employment and banking information. The more current this information is, the more likely you will be able to collect if you ever have to go to eviction court. I'll talk more about that later.

4. Rental/Eviction History

Speaking of evictions, rental and eviction history is the last main criteria to check when screening a tenant, and it's one of the most important. A filed eviction is public record and can be found rather easily with a search on the city's municipal court website. Even an eviction that was filed but dismissed will show there and should be factored in. My company has a hard and fast rule that we do not rent to prospects who have any filed evictions on their record in the past twelve months. If they have one eviction between one and five years ago, we require double the security deposit. Anyone with just one filed eviction over five years we would consider renting to. Applicants with more than one eviction during this timeframe will not be approved.

Evictions are a clear alert of high risk tenants. An eviction typically means a tenant didn't pay their rent, was notified rent was late, had a notice posted regarding late payment, was served a court order to appear, and a judge found them in violation. Most tenants who are going through challenges and need help with a payment plan are usually good about reaching out to the landlord or management company to discuss it. We understand things happen, but when there is little to no communication and someone allows an eviction on their record, they are more likely to repeat the behavior than not. Take evictions on someone's record seriously, and place this criteria as high priority.

In addition, check how long someone has lived at their previous residence; the longer, the better. A prospect provides contact information for at least their last two residences. This could be a private landlord or an apartment complex. Talk to the reference directly and ask questions to 1) confirm what a tenant has included on their application—length of time they lived there, amount of rent paid, and if payments were on time; and 2) confirm intangibles such as how well the tenant kept the place, were there any issues with them, and would you rent to them again. If someone had been living with a family member or friend, it can be trickier to verify this information as family and friends tend to be partial to the tenant and may not provide the most accurate account of what the prospect is like.

So, these are my top screening criteria with income, job history, and eviction record being the top three. I do want to be clear that no screening is foolproof. I've had people who looked great on paper and checked all the boxes but turned out to be the worst tenants ever. On the flip side, I've had tenants that were borderline, who I took a chance on, be some of my best tenants. There's no fail safe here. Over time it becomes easier to spot the red flags, but just understand you may not get it right every time.

FAIR HOUSING

When screening tenants, it's important to not violate any fair housing laws. This is a non-negotiable for any property manager or management company you hire. I recall a sales call with an investor from California who proceeded to tell me he was vehemently against renting his property to any homosexuals and nonchalantly used other homophobic slurs to describe them. He was dead serious. His candor honestly took me by surprise because he was so comfortable telling me this. I quickly let him know that it is not only against our company policy but very much against the law to discriminate based on sexual orientation or gender identity. Needless to say, I didn't agree to work with him. Remember, if you hire a property management company, they are bound to these laws and held to a higher standard and cannot violate them.

Other protected classes include race, color, sex, national origin, religion, disability, and familial status. I find a lot of people are unaware that familial status is on the list. I've had investors tell me they want to only rent to a single person with no kids or someone with only a certain number of kids. This is a discrimination as well.

PETS

Establish your pet policy ahead of time. Anyone who knows me knows I'm not a big pet guy, but I must take into consideration that many people have pets they often treat like family. You can choose whether you want to allow a tenant to have pets in your property or not. You can choose to only allow certain pets or a certain number of pets. There are no restrictions here and completely up to you unless the property management company has a set of rules in your agreement that you must follow. For my company, the general rule is a tenant is allowed up to two dogs (no more than 50lbs combined weight) or two cats, but they are required to put down an upfront, nonrefundable pet fee. These funds are then available to replace carpet or repair floors or any other damage found when the tenant leaves, because trust me, most people who have pets will add wear and tear to your property. Any dog must be a breed that is not on the city's restricted list so learn which ones are. We do not allow any dogs, only cats, for our multi-family homes. When you are dealing with multiple tenants, dogs can often be the primary source of conflict. Either the dog is too loud, or the tenant is picking up after the dog, or, even worse, the tenant is letting the dog shit inside the basement. And typically, multi-family units are not large enough to accommodate too many dogs. It becomes one big headache.

If you choose to allow pets, write it into the lease agreement or pet addendum that you will come to the property quarterly, semi-annually—however often you see fit—for a walkthrough to make sure the property is being kept in good condition. As I mentioned before, pets can add wear and tear to your property and are usually the main reason for damage. As a tenant is unlikely to report damage, the walkthrough will help you keep on top of it. Also confirm tenants are adhering to the number of pets allowed in their agreement. I had a tenant who had been renting a property of mine for about three months and was allowed two cats per her lease. When I went by the house for a check-in, I couldn't believe my eyes. There were cats everywhere, at least a dozen, and in a short 90 days, what was a newly renovated house now looked like a tornado plowed through it. I kid you not, I nearly stepped on this huge cat that, at first glance, I thought was dead. When I looked closer, I could hear him struggle to produce every short, faint, wheezy, breath he made with great effort. This lady was out of control and had to go.

TENANT RELATIONS

If you've been taking notes so far, the next few pages are where you'll really want to put your pen to work. These tips can help you keep tenants happy and ultimately keep them in your property longer.

Maintenance must be your top priority because it will be the top priority for your tenants. Remember, tenants really value safety and want to live in a home that is safe and well maintained. Respond quickly to service calls, and make sure repairs are handled in a timely manner. This is what tenants really want most. Stay on top of and take pride in maintenance, and you'll position yourself to have content, long-term tenants.

When I first started investing and had just a few rental properties of my own, I wanted to standout as a landlord. I wanted to do things other landlords weren't doing for their tenants, especially in the urban market. I used to have welcome baskets waiting for new tenants when they moved in, accompanied with a bouquet of flowers or a nice plant, and I would also send birthday cards on their birthdays and their kids birthdays. I wanted to make them feel special. And they would love it. But you know what they didn't love? The times when I couldn't get a service request completed quickly. All of that "feeling special" went out the window, and my heartfelt gestures were negated by my failure to understand a tenant's top priority. They turned from nice, sweet tenants to angry and upset tenants. Keep on top of maintenance, and you'll keep a happy tenant.

One property I owned had a long-term tenant who lived there for many years. Because she had been such a great tenant, I wanted to do something nice for her. I reached out to let her know how much I appreciated her on time rent payments and keeping up the property over the years. I then presented her with an offer: she could choose one upgrade that I would complete for the house. I gave her the choice of new flooring in the kitchen or bathroom, new faucets, new paint in one or two rooms, or a new toilet. It was the perfect marriage of showing the tenant I cared yet giving her a sense of ownership in the property—all while making updates to my asset. Offer things a tenant would like but you already know the property could use rather than leaving it an open-ended option. Give a few options that are within your budget.

The first time I did this was around the Christmas holiday season, and I continued the tradition each year. I later coined this the "Christmas Surprise." I would plan early in the year and start setting aside money so I'd be ready to make the updates at the end of the year. This helped keep tenants longer and better plan out capital investments into my properties.

One thing to keep in mind is not doing any major projects until a tenant has moved out. Renovating an entire kitchen or bath or fully repainting a house can be challenging while a tenant is living there. Reserve those for unit turnovers, and also refer back to the strategies in the *Preparing Your Property* section of this book. Build upgrades into your budget and updates to the property on an annual basis. This will help preserve your asset and make it more appealing to tenants.

SYSTEMS AND PROCESSES

If you initially manage your properties yourself, set up systems and processes from the onset so you can be consistent with each tenant and property. It will become overwhelming and too difficult to manage if you start making different rules for each tenant. I'd also suggest never collecting rent in person. In fact, the less the tenant knows you as the owner of the property the better. Preserve your anonymity as much as possible. A tenant will respect your interactions with them on a more professional and business level if they see you as an employee for the "property management company." The second they know you own the property, their demeanor tends to change and they look at you differently.

I used to collect rent directly from my tenants each month, and they knew I was the property owner. I drove a black Lincoln Navigator with nice trim and chrome wheels. You could see me coming from a mile away. I often left straight from work and would arrive in my dress shoes, slacks, and collared shirt;

my tenants thought I was rich, looking like Jordan Belfort, and I certainly wasn't. But perception is everything. I show up asking for money, and they think I've already got enough. I was seen as a greedy and impassive landlord, leading tenants to pick and choose when they wanted to pay rent—because in their minds, I'd be fine even if the rent was late. The tenants saw me simply as someone taking their money rather than them paying to keep a roof over their heads. It became too personal and proved to be detrimental to my business. This was over fifteen years ago, when collecting rent in person was more commonplace, but the experience taught me a lot and I altered my practices.

With modern day technology, rent collection is much easier. A system can be set up where tenants pay via a bank transfer or pay app such as PayPal, Venmo, or Zelle. I highly suggest setting up a business entity and having everything tie to your business bank accounts. Remove yourself from the rent collection process all together. Be firm on when rent is due, and if rent is late, place a three-day notice on their door. Maintain the same process every month and for every tenant. Have a convenient way for tenants to request service calls, and have a team of contractors and vendors ready to go. Have a process for managing unruly or difficult tenants. How will you handle tenant complaints? Will you set up a main number for them to call, or will they have to email or submit complaints through a website? Really take time to decide on processes, and put them in writing for your own reference. Remember, as you grow your investments, these processes will evolve over time.

Now, the easiest way to implement this, and what I highly recommend, is to hire a property management company rather than tackling it all on your own. Most companies already have specific processes and systems in place, so ask questions to understand how they operate. Best practice is to avoid direct contact with tenants as much as possible. Even with a property management company in place, I've seen too many owners still call tenants or drop by the properties unannounced. Leave this all to the management company.

RENT & EVICTIONS

All tenants know rent is due the first of every month. This should never be a surprise to them. But it's inevitable that, at some point in your investing career, you will have a tenant who does not pay on time or perhaps even pay at all. This happens more often in the urban market than in A&B markets, largely because of the intrinsic low economic conditions and lower paying jobs. Unemployment rates tend to be higher, and tenants tend to switch jobs more frequently. You must prepare yourself for nonpaying tenants.

Having a vacant property is the biggest problem you will have as an out-of-state investor in an urban market. It makes you vulnerable to theft, vandalism, and all kinds of mechanical failures. In colder climates, a vacant property needs to be winterized to protect it from the catastrophic damage frozen pipes create when they burst. One way avoid vacancy (and to keep tenants paying rent) is to avoid rent increases as long as possible. In the urban market, a long-term tenant paying below-market rent, consistently on time, is extremely valuable. I highly encourage you leave the rent at the current rate or only raise it slightly—no more than 10%. Increasing rent from $700 to $725 per month is more palatable than going from $700 to $800 per month, for example. Time and again, when I've seen owners raise rents by a considerable amount, tenants typically push back and leave. Most have fixed incomes and can't absorb high swings in their monthly expenses. You're left with a vacant unit, no rental income, and several thousand dollars in turnover costs. Rather than the additional $100 per month you wanted, yielding $1200 per year, you could instead be out a month's worth of rent and on average a minimum of $2,000 turnover costs preparing the property to rent again, not to mention the leasing fee. Consider whether it's worth that risk. Be prepared to add clean out costs as a large part of the turnover budget as well. Many investors are surprised by tenants who take nothing with them—they'll leave everything from beds, dressers, and tables to other belongings scattered throughout the property, inside and outside. This is common. You now have to pay someone to remove the belongings and properly dispose of them. Again, we are talking about lower-income families who aren't always afforded the convenience of renting a U-Haul and buying expensive moving boxes so they can properly pack up their things and leave. For many, it's easier to leave everything behind and start over at their new place. So, remember, when you have a good paying tenant and are thinking about raising the rent, it's best most times to leave well enough alone.

 If you still decide to raise the rent, give the tenant at least a 30-to 90-day notice of the rent increase, and increase only slightly to keep a paying tenant in the property. This can also be a good time to re-verify a tenant's income. A tenant may agree to a rent increase they cannot afford but will then look for another place before the increase takes effect. In the urban market, a better time to increase rent is while marketing the unit for a new tenant. It's much easier to make the change at the onset of a lease.

My three golden rules which are **1) no drastic changes to the rent amount; 2) handle all requested work orders promptly; and 3) keep the property safe and updated.** Even still, you may have a non-paying tenant at some point and wind up in eviction court. It's likely inevitable if you invest in the urban real estate market long-term. Maintain the same process each month and stay consistent with each tenant. Once you start making exceptions, tenants will take advantage every time.

Most investors consider eviction their first and only option to handle a non-paying tenant. I suggest first determining why a tenant is not paying. Perhaps their financial situation has changed and they need assistance. Providing resources for rental assistance programs could help a tenant get back on their feet. It also ensures you keep receiving rent payments. There are typically more of these types of programs available in the urban market.

Most tenants will not want an eviction on their record and will entertain alternative options if you will work with them. In addition, in many cities the formal eviction process can take, on average, 30 to 90 days, depending on local housing court. In the urban market, many judges and magistrates lean more on the side of the tenant than landlord, which can prolong the process even more. Imagine having a tenant not pay rent for months, and you finally get in front of a judge to evict them only to have the judge be sympathetic to the fact the tenant has children. The case could be continued for a few more weeks, granting the tenant access to free counsel from the legal aid society. That's additional time without rent. It can be a very long process.

A formal eviction process will involve attorney and court fees, but it most often results in the tenant leaving on their own before the process is completed. Either way, the tenant is out.

Collecting your losses from the tenant is another thing though. Considering the transient employment many tenants have, and many don't have traditional bank accounts, attempts to garnish wages may be futile even with a court order.

As an investor in the urban market, also be prepared for tenants to leave without notice in the middle of a lease. This takes many landlords by surprise. For various reasons, a tenant may not uphold their lease agreement. Many will if you've followed my three golden rules, but it's usually when one of these rules isn't followed that a tenant chooses to leave. They aren't worried about their security deposit and won't even bother to request it back. Most will consider it their last month's rent payment instead. And good luck tracking them down. It's just one of the unfortunate realities of the urban real estate market.

INSPECTIONS

It's important to stay on top of required city inspections or voucher program inspections related to your property. It's also a good idea to create an annual or semi-annual schedule to check the major systems in the property, such as the furnace, and ensure smoke and carbon monoxide detectors are installed and properly working.

What's not a good idea is showing up unannounced on a regular basis to "check up" on tenants for the purpose of inspecting the property. I often get investors who believe this is something they should or are supposed to do; I highly discourage it. Understand that normal wear and tear will occur as it does in any house. Yes, you own the property and have every right to it; however, it is still your tenant's home, and their rent payment entitles them to respect and privacy to an extent. There's no need for routine inspections, but use your discretion.

I once had a property with a tenant who had lived there for a couple of years, paid their rent on time, and I'd had no trouble from them. They placed a rare service call one day, and when the maintenance tech went in, the place was in complete disarray. There was dog shit everywhere—from a dog they were not supposed to have—kitchen cabinet doors were missing, a blade on a ceiling fan was broken, and the dog had chewed away at the back door. And can you imagine the smell? By anyone's standards, this was more than normal wear and tear. The tenant was given a formal warning for breaking their lease agreement, which stated they were not to have pets and were expected to keep the home in good condition. I also charged them for the repairs. Fortunately, I didn't have problems from them again.

In this case, I didn't plan an inspection; but if you do annual inspections or take service calls, it's a great opportunity to check in on your properties. If you see any violations, regular inspections become warranted to ensure the tenant keeps things in order. If they continue to breach the rules, you may have just cause to give them notice to leave.

Overall, if a tenant is paying their rent on time and not being a nuisance, the best advice is to let them be. General rule, it's YOUR HOUSE, but it's THEIR HOME.

SUMMARY

Tenants are the heartbeat of your asset. Your ability to merge a business mindset with a human approach will set you apart. How well you preserve your asset is important to most tenants and should be your objective as well. The more you ensure the property is safe and comfortable for your tenant, the greater your chance of having positive tenant relations. Think of it as a mirror. The condition of your attitude and property is often a direct reflection of the occupancy rates and quality of tenant you will attract. What's helps is asking "Would I live here?"—not based on the style of home or the aesthetics, but on common human decency.

Tenants are a variable you can't always predict. Navigating tenants in the urban market especially will require having systems and processes in place. Firm systems breed consistency for those who occupy your asset. Understand the history of distrust urban market tenants have with landlords and be sensitive to it. You need them. They don't need you. Understanding their challenges helps you provide a service that keeps your asset cash flowing.

CHAPTER SIX

Building A Team

Building a team with the right key players is paramount to success in real estate investing. If you're an out-of-state investor, you will need a team even more. This team will consist of people who bring together different skill sets to aid in your success. In sports, for instance, each player has their individual sets of skills, but they come together as a team to reach a common goal.

The Chicago Bulls in the '90s were a perfect depiction of what a team should be. I remember like it was yesterday, growing up right outside of Chicago, I was a huge Chicago Bulls fan. And at that time, who wasn't? They dominated the game for nearly a decade. It was spectacular to witness. The Chicago Bulls and Michael Jordan were everything to me back then and to the entire city. We called them the UnstoppaBulls. Each night they played united the city.

The Chicago Bulls were an incredible team brought together by head coach Phil Jackson. ESPN released a docuseries on Netflix titled *The Last Dance* which chronicled the rise of the Bulls and Jackson's leadership. Everyone wondered how he put such an incredible team together because each man on the team had his peculiar personality and skills, and yet they all fit together like a jigsaw puzzle. They were all positioned strategically across the court based on their strengths; no one ever stood in another's place. Jackson was able to take his team to six championships—a mind blowing feat. As you build your team, think of yourself as the head coach, selecting the right players to win a championship.

Should you choose to hire a property manager, they become the head coach, so to speak, and you become the team owner. Most often, the property manager will already have a powerhouse team established that you can utilize. But don't make the rookie mistake of just sitting back and relaxing, thinking your head coach will take care of everything without any of your involvement. Remember, you're still the team owner, so you handle the high-level operations and let your property manager handle the day-to-day. Make sure you're briefed on a regular basis and always know what is going on with your property. Understand what repairs are needed, if tenants are paying or not, and any issues that may arise. Stay informed. There is an overwhelming amount of trust needed between you and your property manager. However, if you want to verify that things are being done, don't hesitate to ask for photos or video of completed work. I've even had some owners go as far as sending someone over to the property for a second confirmation a job was completed, which I applaud. Take whatever measures are needed for you to feel comfortable.

At the end of the day, great communication from your property manager makes all the difference. This quality tends to be lacking in many companies in the urban market, so when you find a transparent management company with great communication, you're golden. Vet a property manager to learn their communication style. Get referrals or ask the company directly for contact information of owners they work with to get a firsthand account based on owners' experiences. Another great litmus test is understanding the company's policies and procedures. If they can't explain these in great detail and/or have them clearly written for review, you may want to continue your search for another property manager.

A good property manager can also act as a consultant, advising on how to protect your asset and potentially grow your portfolio. But don't expect a partnership with all of the reward and none of the liability. This is where the lines often get blurred. It's important to manage your expectations of the property management company. They are not miracle workers, and I find my investors often think they should be. Property managers are often tasked to handle a lot, and for an industry standard 10% fee, in the urban market it can average to just $70 per month per unit.

Hiring a property manager does not free you of the inherent risks of investing, especially in the urban market. For example, whether a tenant always pays rent is not within their control. They don't always know why a tenant hasn't paid, but a good property manager will have processes in place to handle these situations. That's the best they can do.

I was having a conversation with an investor who hired my company to manage her property. We had been marketing her property for a new tenant for a few weeks, and there were some showings but no applications. All of the feedback indicated there was an abandoned house next door, and many saw it as a safety concern. This was something outside of our control, but she didn't want to lower the rent amount as we advised, or add additional exterior security features such as more lighting to help better market the property. Again, expectations must be managed. We consulted her the best we could, but she did not want to share the responsibility of fixing the problem by making adjustments.

There are often misconceptions about property managers. Many think all they do is place tenants in vacant units, collect rent, and take a few phone calls. There are many variables a property manager experiences on a daily basis, especially in the urban real estate market. In real estate, there are many ups and downs and unpredictable factors. There's usually some type of conflict or problem that must be resolved. Nonpaying tenants need to be evicted or contractors don't follow through on completing work and now a repair is delayed. People are often the biggest variable in the equation. Property managers are really managing people and unpredictable variables more than they are physically managing your property. It's a difficult job in the urban market, and it's why the vast majority of people are happy to hand that job over to property managers.

THE DRAFT

Now that you've got a property manager, it's time to compile your team. Here is a list of the key players you'll need on your roster.

1. Real Estate Agent
2. Contractors and Handymen

3. Public or Traditional Lenders
4. Local Officials
5. Real Estate Attorney
6. Accountant
7. Financial Advisor

REAL ESTATE AGENT

I've already talked about the importance of a great real estate agent, but here are few key points to remember.

Expectations for the Relationship

- Make sure your agent has strong knowledge and experience in the urban real estate market and can navigate its complexities well. This is important. Not all agents are created equal when it comes to this market. Choose wisely.

How to Maintain the Relationship

- Real estate agents are licensed professionals; treat them as such. They have taken classes and tests to obtain their license, and they take continuing education classes to keep it. Agents know more than the average person when it comes to real estate and how it works. They are held to a higher standard and a code of ethics as well. Treat them with respect and be respectful of their time. Don't bounce from agent to agent. Build a strong relationship with one.
- How to Find a Real Estate Agent

- Get referrals from other investors, your property management company, or your network.
- Search to see which agents are doing sales in the market you are targeting.
- Search Google and Zillow agent reviews.

CONTRACTORS AND HANDYMEN

Believe me when I say this, many contractors have a reputation for being liars, snakes, and thieves. In over fifteen years in the urban market, I've come across many. Contractors can often be the biggest source of the headaches you'll experience. It's unfortunate, but finding good, go-to contractors to add to your team will be the hardest spot on your roster to fill.

Expectations for the Relationship

- I've often found contractors to lack time management, communication, and administrative skills. Many can do their job well, but when you factor in these skills, they can't seem to bring the entire picture together. Many are a product of the urban real estate environment you're investing in. They don't understand the business side to what they do and more or less hustle their way through.
- Contractors who lack business savvy and time management skills will overbook themselves, promising to be in five places at once and to complete all jobs at the same time. It's unrealistic, but they see the dollar signs and tend to overpromise and underdeliver. If that happens, someone will need to make sure they show up at the job each day on time and are actually working.

- Sometimes it's best to find different skilled trade workers rather than just one general contractor. You'll likely get better quality work, and done more efficiently, when you have skilled trade workers come in for smaller projects when needed.

- Understand you get what you pay for. Many investors want to cut costs and go with the lowest priced contractor, but this is where a lot of their headaches arise. They find themselves having to hire someone else to come behind a contractor who did a sloppy and incomplete job, costing them more money in the end. Contractors who are more polished and professional will charge more, but you may find it money well spent. Getting two to three quotes can help you best understand what pricing makes the most sense.

- Also make sure your contractor is licensed and bonded. While this can be more difficult to find in the urban market, it's worth having as a goal, at least for your large projects.

How to Maintain the Relationship

- This relationship can be very fluid and difficult to establish long term. One minute you have a contractor who you've worked with on a few projects and has met all expectations, and the next minute you never hear from them again. It comes with the territory, particularly in the urban real estate market.

- Building trust with contractors will take time. Be clear about your expectations up front, and stay firm on them. When a contractor gives me a timeline for work completion, I confirm repeatedly whether they are sure they can meet that deadline. Usually they respond three times with a "yes." At that point, I propose that if the work is not done by one week past that due date, I start deducting a certain dollar amount from what I've agreed to pay. The contractor who has no problem with it is the one I usually go with.

- When talking to a contractor about his price if they ever say "For You," beware. "What's your price for repairing this gutter?" *"For you..."* "What's your price for changing this outlet?" *"For You..."* Why for me? They don't even know me. This is a telltale sign of a contractor you need to run from. Anyone who is quick to give you "discounts" when you haven't yet established a relationship with is not the right contractor. This tells me they are thirsty for business or don't know how to estimate their work. I've found many will come to me in the middle of a project asking for more money because they didn't budget for enough, or some will just abandon a project in the middle of it for the same reason.

- Keeping your end of the bargain is part of maintaining a good relationship with your contractor. Trust is a two-way street, and they need to know you'll pay them on time and in full when a job is complete. It's a lot easier to hold them accountable when you show up on time, have materials ready to go, and do what you say you're going to do.

How to Find a Contractor

- Focus on referrals as much as you can. You could search online or Craigslist as a last resort, but make sure to get references.

- If you use a property manager, and they will have contractors they typically work with. In this case, you won't have much control over pricing and should expect to pay a small markup.

Pro Tip: Buy Materials Yourself

Having control over the material costs is to your benefit if you understand what is needed. It's fairly easy to establish a Pro Account at Home Depot or Lowe's that can be used nationwide. You can order materials directly, and the materials will be delivered right to the site. This will prove to be both time and cost effective as it will alleviate the time contractors spend obtaining materials and eliminate any extra costs they may bill you for. Trust me, those add up

PRIVATE OR TRADITIONAL LENDERS

Lenders are critical to get deals done, and the type of lender depends on your particular needs and goals.

Expectations for the Relationship

- This relationship is usually one of your longest as you'll often still with a good lender and grow your investments.
- Be organized and prepared on your end. The lender can help facilitate getting you necessary funds, but they can't

gather your documents, file your tax returns, or keep track of your finances for you.

How to Maintain the Relationship

- Keep the lines of communication open. Let your lender know of your needs and how they can help.

- Be honest and upfront. If you are having challenges, it's best to discuss it with your lender. They can't help what they don't know about. A traditional lender will find out anyway, so don't hold anything back.

- Maintain a good standing by paying lenders on time, especially private lenders where the relationship is usually a closer one. Factor in vacancy rates and potential repairs to ensure you can make payments on time. The quickest way to ruin this relationship and create a bad reputation for yourself is to blemish your integrity.

How to Find a Traditional or Private Lender

- Your real estate agent will likely be your best resource.

- For private lenders, don't be afraid to make it known to just about anyone you come in contact with that you're looking for financing opportunities. You might be surprised who may be able to connect you.

LOCAL OFFICIALS

The importance of this relationship has been undervalued and underutilized. Remember that high government compliance is one of the three identifiers of the urban market. There will be government and city entities you'll have to work with, and it's a good idea to get to know the right people in these departments. When I refer to local officials, it includes magistrates and housing court workers, city building and housing directors, inspectors and city councilmen, mayors and state reps. These are relationships worth developing now for the help they can provide later.

There's a local municipality right outside of Cleveland that is notorious for not being investor friendly. Because my company manages a large number of properties in that area, our name has shown up often regarding evictions or violations. As a result, it appeared as though my company owned many properties and was seen as an absentee foreign investor. We unwittingly assumed a bad reputation, and the magistrates and other officials made things very difficult for us. This is where having a strong network can help. I had a friend whose husband worked for the city. He did me a favor and put me in touch with the city's housing director. I was able to set up a meeting with the director to discuss my company's role as property manager and our efforts in working with owners. I explained we do not own the properties but act as a conduit. That conversation helped resolve a number of misunderstandings and turned things around tremendously.

Expectations for the Relationship
- The more properties you own in an area, the more beneficial it will be to get to know the local officials. When you are starting out it may not be a priority, but keep it in mind.

- Some may look at this a schmoozing, and I'm here to tell you it is. To a certain extent. It can a bad thing if you're trying to manipulate people, but to develop the relationships is important. Just like with any relationship, you want to nurture it, and doing a little more than the norm will help it grow. Such as when I give flowers to Lisa, my children's daycare director, as a thank you for taking such great care of them; or when I pass along a bottle of water to Ben, my garbage man, for making sure no trash gets left in the street. Or when I leave random notes in my mailbox for Lindsay, my mail lady, just letting her know she's appreciated. It's the little things.

How to Maintain the Relationship

- If you are local, attending city council meetings is a great place to start. You'll be able to see and meet officials on a weekly basis, and they will see and get to know you in return. You'll hear about the city's plans and proposals for development, housing, ordinances, and more. These meetings will be very beneficial to you as an investor.

- As you get to know some of the officials, offer to take them to lunch or coffee. Provide them with feedback on improvements for the area or concerns you may have. Make it a constructive meeting with something tangible they can leave with, all while building rapport and establishing a relationship.

- Once you a familiar with the officials, consider making donations to their campaigns or charity events. This is a way to get noticed and stay top of mind, especially if you are able to make significant contributions.

- A simple thank you goes a long way. If a housing inspector did a favor for you, send a card or edible arrangement. If you find yourself in housing court, always smile and say hello. Remember, we are talking about government offices here, so it's usually a very somber environment. A warm smile and a "How are you doing?" will get noticed.

REAL ESTATE ATTORNEY

Having a good real estate attorney is like that sixth man on your team. You don't need them all the time, but when you need them in the game they will deliver. For my NBA basketball fans, think of Robert Horry. He played for a few teams and was instrumental in hitting those clutch baskets to help pull his team to victory.

Make sure you identify and vet a real estate attorney. Most attorneys have different disciplines, so you may work with several. You'll want attorney that does evictions, one to help structure and close deals or contracts, and one that can represent you in the event of legal trouble if a tenant or someone sues you.

Also, understand the state and areas you are investing in. Some states require title work and the escrow process be handled by a closing attorney. Some states require the title work and escrow be handled by a title company and not an attorney. Whether it's a closing attorney or a title company, it's a good idea to establish a strong relationship because some will lower their fees after a significant amount of business has been done together. Also, when all of your deals are through one company, they'll have your information already for ease of the next deal. It's also easy and efficient to obtain paperwork for taxes if you only have one place to go through.

One positive is I haven't met any fly-by-night attorneys. They're typically consistent, very knowledgeable, and stay in their profession for decades. This relationship will be another one you'll want to establish for the long haul.

Expectations for the Relationship

- If you are working with a property management company, they likely have attorneys they already work with and a process for evictions.

- In some jurisdictions, if you own a property under an LLC, you will need an attorney to represent you for evictions.

- To have an attorney available in case of lawsuits or for contracts or other legal advice, it may be worth establishing a retainer so they know you are serious and will be ready to go when you need them. Some eviction attorneys may require a retainer, but many will bill per case.

How to Maintain the Relationship

- Referrals are always appreciated so send some as often as you can.

- Pay your attorney fees on time.

- Trust and follow their advice. They are the experts.

How to Find a Real Estate Attorney

- Word of mouth, referrals from your real estate agent or property management company, or attending investor meet up groups are your best resources.

- Search the housing court website for current or old hearings. This is all public record. Oftentimes the name of the attorney or firm who represented the client is listed. Do some research and give them a call.

- Attend eviction hearings. You'll often find the same handful of attorneys are representing several clients. Introduce yourself and determine who is a good fit.

ACCOUNTANT

Regardless of how many or few properties you own, an accountant will prove to be extremely valuable. It's one of those people you'll want on your team sooner rather than later. It's easier to establish a system for all of your accounting with a great accountant right from the start and not after the twentieth property purchase.

Expectations for the Relationship

- Your accountant must have a good understanding of the specific type of real estate you are investing in. For instance, residential real estate is very different from commercial. It's best to have an accountant who understands the nuances and tax codes for your niche and the particular state you invest in. Make no exceptions here.

- Your communication and relationship with your accountant is typically more seasonal, but be sure to reach out if questions come up throughout the year. It's good to keep them in the loop regarding your investment plans to ensure plans coincide with your tax strategies. An accountant should advise you and provide tips on how to reduce tax liabilities whenever possible.

- One thing accountants appreciate is having organized clients. Your property manager should provide all of your year-end statements and financials to give to your accountant. Keep in mind, as you grow, you may want to add a bookkeeper to your team as well. A bookkeeper is different than an accountant in that they reconcile your numbers on a monthly basis. Bookkeepers help categorize your expenses and keep track of your numbers. This is not your accountant's job. You can easily do this yourself until it becomes too much to manage on your own. When it comes time to prepare your taxes, take the numbers your bookkeeper recorded all year and submit them to your accountant to file your taxes.

How to Maintain the Relationship

- It is imperative that you have accurate data and record keeping throughout the year. Accountants will appreciate your efforts when they are able to efficiently process your paperwork.

- Send referrals; they'll appreciate it.

How to Find an Accountant

- I can categorically say that the best accountants usually come through referrals from friends, family, other investors, your real estate agent, meet up groups, you name it. Don't just get someone off Google. Get a referral. Talk to others who have used that accountant. Get social proof of their performance. Accountants, for the most part, can all do the same thing. What will set each apart is their communication style, personality, and experience. It's good to meet with a few accountants before deciding on one to make sure he or she is a good fit with your communication style and personality. Do you need someone who is patient, a good listener, and will walk you through everything and really teach you about tax strategy? Or do you want someone who gives it to you straight, no chaser? Understand what you need and be able to articulate it.

FINANCIAL ADVISOR

I spoke in depth about wealth and freedom mindset earlier in the book. One thing I've learned is that it's hard to achieve what you haven't planned for. As the saying goes, "If you fail to plan, you plan to fail." I'm not sure who is behind that quote, but it's always stuck with me. To reach your financial goals, real estate related and beyond, I highly suggest having a financial advisor on your team. They will work with you to create a comprehensive view of your financial plan that includes all aspects of your life, not just for real estate. An advisor can help you grow your portfolio of stocks, bonds, and mutual funds. They will help you budget and save for emergencies, education, and plan for retirement. They will show you how to protect your assets and ensure you have proper insurance. Financial advisors can help you create a legacy for your children and future generations.

Expectations for the Relationship

- There is a level of vulnerability you will need to have with your financial advisor. You will be discussing subjects that can be very personal and sensitive for some. Talking about money isn't always easy, but be open and honest for the best results.

- You will want to have a strong level of trust with your financial advisor. They should keep your information and discussions confidential. It's important that you are honest regarding your desires and challenges so they can best help you meet your financial goals. Understand that this trust isn't always immediate and can take time to nurture.

How to Maintain the Relationship

- When you first begin working with a financial advisor, you may have to meet on a regular basis to establish a plan and begin to execute it. Once you've moved past the initial phase, meet with your advisor either quarterly, semi-annually, or annually. This will depend on your needs and plan but at the very least meet once a year.

- Follow their advice and respect their time.

How to Find a Financial Advisor

- By now I sound like a broken record, but get a referral, referral, referral. Enough said.

SUMMARY

Anything I've achieved in my life is a result of working well with others. Your human resources will be your greatest attribute. You'll find people are often willing to help and will believe in what you're doing. Harness that energy and the horsepower that goes with it. Most of that horsepower will come from your property manager. Know how everyone will fit together and the roles each play. The most important part is not only finding the right people but maintaining relationships. Remember, relationships are a two-way street. It's not about adding players based on what they can do for you. You must work together to achieve your goals. As the old saying goes, Cuando trabajamos juntos ganamos mas. (Look it up, bitch.)

CHAPTER SEVEN

Conclusion

I have three main, overarching takeaways to leave you with. The first is, you did not buy an annuity. An annuity is a long-term investment designed to give you financial security and protect you from the risk of outliving your income through a series of payments made to you at equal intervals. Unfortunately, this is not what investing in real estate is. I have seen many investors who bought properties in an urban market with the mindset that they purchased an annuity. They believe so strongly that they do not have to be actively involved, just hire someone to manage the property and receive consistent monthly payments with no problems. There's much more to it, and I want to drive this point home. I hope I've successfully illustrated the many variables and nuances of the urban real estate market.

Second, always continue to grow. Stay on top of your research, market trends, rent rates, and industry knowledge. Stay connected to the ever-changing technology that can bring efficiency and cost savings. There will be ebbs and flows to investing, so prepare and educate yourself as much as possible. Always be a student.

Lastly, my number one goal with this book is to help and educate novice investors of the urban real estate market. I have spent nearly two decades learning, growing, and making mistakes in this market. Being a property manager has blessed me with the opportunity to see urban real estate investment from a variety of angles. I'm truly thankful because it allows me to be empathetic and knowledgeable, and provide solutions for all the challenges that are presented and the multitude of aspects of this industry. No one gets ahead alone. At the end of the day, I am your guide. I want to be on your team, as small as my part may be, to help achieve your goals. Mark this moment as the beginning of the legacy you will leave. In the words of my late dear friend and mentor, Rich Clark, "It's what we ought to be doing."

www.ingramcontent.com/pod-product-compliance
Lightning Source LLC
Chambersburg PA
CBHW061944220426
43662CB00012B/2016